Frommer's®

Portable
Turks & Caicos

3rd Edition

by Alexis Lipsitz Flippin

WILEY
Wiley Publishing, Inc.

Published by:

WILEY PUBLISHING, INC.

111 River St.
Hoboken, NJ 07030-5774

ISBN 978-0-470-63098-3 (paper); ISBN 978-0-470-92885-1 (ebk); ISBN
978-0-470-92886-8 (ebk); ISBN 978-0-470-92887-5 (ebk)

Editor: Jamie Ehrlich
Production Editor: Eric T. Schroeder
Cartographer: Anton Crane
Photo Editor: Richard Fox
Production by Wiley Indianapolis Composition Services

Front cover photo: A heron on the shore at Little Waters Cay. ©Tim Cuff /
Alamy Images.

For information on our other products and services or to obtain technical
support, please contact our Customer Care Department within the U.S. at
877/762-2974, outside the U.S. at 317/572-3993 or fax 317/572-4002.

Wiley also publishes its books in a variety of electronic formats. Some con-
tent that appears in print may not be available in electronic formats.

Manufactured in the United States of America

5   4   3   2   1

CONTENTS

TURKS & CAICOS

CONTENTS

LIST OF MAPS

ABOUT THE AUTHOR

Alexis Lipsitz Flippin is a former Frommer's Senior Editor and the author of *Frommer's St. Martin, St. Barts & Anguilla* and *Frommer's NYC with Kids* and a coauthor of *Frommer's 500 Extraordinary Islands*. She has written and edited for consumer magazines and websites such as *Self, American Health,* CNN.com, Weather.com, and *Rolling Stone*.

ACKNOWLEDGMENTS

I'd like to thank the following individuals for their enormous help and support, in no particular order: the Turks & Caicos Tourist Board; Karen Whitt and Scott Hagan, the Somerset on Grace Bay; Dane Underwood, the West Bay Club; Grant Friedman and Jean Francois Tremblay, the Gansevoort Turks + Caicos; Jeff Morgan, Parrot Cay; Nikheel Advani, Thierry Grandsire, and Anthony Johnson, the Grace Bay Club; Beverly Williams, the Regent Grand; the Regent Palms; the Veranda; Katrina Birt and Sandy Erb, Grand Turk Inn; Porter Williams, Island Thyme Bistro; and Debbie Been, Salt Cay Divers.

HOW TO CONTACT US

In researching this book, we discovered many wonderful places—hotels, restaurants, shops, and more. We're sure you'll find others. Please tell us about them, so we can share the information with your fellow travelers in upcoming editions. If you were disappointed with a recommendation, we'd love to know that, too. Please write to:

Frommer's Portable Turks & Caicos, 3rd Edition
Wiley Publishing, Inc. • 111 River St. • Hoboken, NJ 07030-5774
frommersfeedback@wiley.com

AN ADDITIONAL NOTE

Please be advised that travel information is subject to change at any time—and this is especially true of prices. We therefore suggest that you write or call ahead for confirmation when making your travel plans. The authors, editors, and publisher cannot be held responsible for the experiences of readers while traveling. Your safety is important to us, however, so we encourage you to stay alert and be aware of your surroundings. Keep a close eye on cameras, purses, and wallets, all favorite targets of thieves and pickpockets.

FROMMER'S STAR RATINGS, ICONS & ABBREVIATIONS

Every hotel, restaurant, and attraction listing in this guide has been ranked for quality, value, service, amenities, and special features using a **star-rating system.** In country, state, and regional guides, we also rate towns and regions to help you narrow down your choices and budget your time accordingly. Hotels and restaurants are rated on a scale of zero (recommended) to three stars (exceptional). Attractions, shopping, nightlife, towns, and regions are rated according to the following scale: zero stars (recommended), one star (highly recommended), two stars (very highly recommended), and three stars (must-see).

In addition to the star-rating system, we also use **seven feature icons** that point you to the great deals, in-the-know advice, and unique experiences that separate travelers from tourists. Throughout the book, look for:

(Finds)	Special finds—those places only insiders know about
(Fun Facts)	Fun facts—details that make travelers more informed and their trips more fun
(Kids)	Best bets for kids and advice for the whole family
(Moments)	Special moments—those experiences that memories are made of
(Overrated)	Places or experiences not worth your time or money
(Tips)	Insider tips—great ways to save time and money
(Value)	Great values—where to get the best deals

The following **abbreviations** are used for credit cards:

AE American Express	DISC Discover	V Visa
DC Diners Club	MC MasterCard	

TRAVEL RESOURCES AT FROMMERS.COM

Frommer's travel resources don't end with this guide. **Frommers.com** has travel information on more than 4,000 destinations. We update features regularly, giving you access to the most current trip-planning information and the best airfare, lodging, and car-rental bargains. You can also listen to podcasts, connect with other Frommers.com members through our active-reader forums, share your travel photos, read blogs from guidebook editors and fellow travelers, and much more.

The Best of the Turks & Caicos Islands

For years, the Turks and Caicos Islands' stunning natural attributes were known to just a fortunate few travelers—many of them divers and snorkelers exploring the coral reefs and dramatic drop-offs of the continental shelf wall. But the Turks and Caicos are undiscovered no more: Overnight, it seems, this sun-kissed archipelago has become synonymous with tropical island luxury. A building boom along the 19km (12 miles) of Grace Bay Beach has fashioned a sleek lineup of upscale resort hotels.

The Turks and Caicos Islands (TCI) are a marine paradise, free of pollution and noise. Even with the advent of real tourist development and the bustle of construction—particularly on the main island of Providenciales (nicknamed "Provo")—the beauty and tranquillity of this little island chain remain intact.

What has put Turks and Caicos on the map are the gorgeous beaches—362km (224 miles) of them, to be precise. Some stretches of soft white sand run extraordinary lengths; others are small, tucked into secluded coves. The islands are also home to magnificent underwater life. Countless varieties of brilliant coral and colorful fish thrive within TCI's nearly 800km (496-mile) coral reef system—the world's third-largest.

For many years, this nation of low-lying coral islands just below the Bahamas was little more than a beautiful, slumbering backwater, home to a close-knit society of some 30,000 islanders called Belongers, descendants of black slaves brought to the island by British Loyalists in the late 18th century to work cotton plantations. When cotton went bust as an island crop, the Brits moved on, leaving the slaves behind. So for some 250 years, these freed slaves had the islands pretty much to themselves, save for a sampling of beach bums, sailors, divers, and smugglers. But these beaches and marine wonders weren't going to stay unnoticed for long. A small airstrip was built in the 1960s, Club Med (the island's first resort) arrived in 1984, and in the 1990s development of the high-end variety was being actively encouraged. The islands—especially Provo—quickly became one of the fastest-growing resort destinations in the Caribbean.

In spite of the ramped-up development, this British Overseas Territory has managed to retain a laidback feel; even the upscale resorts have absorbed the warm, whimsical TCI outlook—no attitude here, thank you. If you're looking for scintillating nightlife, however, you'll be sorely disappointed. On the TCI, the island beach-bar-and-barbecue-shack ethos still reigns.

This is not to say that visitors can't get their fill of high-adrenaline outdoor adventures. You can scuba-dive a vertical undersea wall where the continental shelf drops a heart-stopping mile deep (*Scuba Diving* magazine named the TCI one of the top 10 diving sites in the world), swim alongside humpback whales and velvety stingrays, cast a line for bonefish, or free-dive 20 feet to the sea bottom for fresh conch.

For many travelers, however, a visit to the TCI is as much about what you *won't* experience as what you do. You won't hear the constant roar of jet skis (the coral reef is part of a protected national park) or spend your beach time stepping over sunbathers packed like sardines. You don't see giant water parks rising up over the horizon. You aren't confronted by pushy hucksters roaming the beach.

And don't even bother coming if you're looking for a shopping spree. Chain retailers and superstores have yet to make inroads here (the government has a ban on chains of any kind). The mega T-shirt shops that have become ubiquitous in many seaside resorts are nowhere to be found here. You *can* buy T-shirts, for sure, both of the generic tourist variety and more personalized versions, at boutique shops scattered about in the few retail clusters on Provo. You can also find good art by local and regional artists in established galleries. Home furnishing shops are opening in ever-increasing numbers, and luxury brands are sold at upscale resort boutiques.

The lack of chains means no international fast-food outlets. But you can get more than acceptable nonchain burgers, pizzas, and any kind of Western-style grub you desire—as well as some delicious classic island fare, especially in the Blue Hills area. We're talking conch, fish, curries, and peas 'n' rice. Expect to pay bruising big-city prices most everywhere you go, however; little grows in this parched, sandy terrain and, aside from local seafood, much has to be flown in daily.

Indeed, if you like your Caribbean islands thrillingly lush and mountainous, the dry scrubland terrain of the TCI may underwhelm you. But if you dream of lying on a beautiful stretch of sugary sand lapped by dazzling bottle-green seas, this is the place for you.

For a thumbnail portrait of each island, see "The Islands in Brief," in chapter 2.

1 THE BEST BEACHES

Surrounded by the world's third-largest coral reef, the Turks and Caicos Islands have some of the finest powdery-sand beaches and most ethereal turquoise seas in the world. Most are just minutes away from an airport, and you'll rarely have to vie for beach space with anyone else. Tour boats can whisk you to uninhabited cays where you can play Robinson Crusoe for a day. The waters are pristine and dia-mond-clear, and waves rarely rise above a gentle ripple—perfect for young kids and snorkelers of all ages.

- **Grace Bay** (Providenciales): These 19km (12 miles) of pale sands and azure seas are the pride of Provo; Grace Bay Beach was named the World's Leading Beach for several years running at the World Travel Awards. An increasing number of resorts and condo hotels have sprung up along the shore. Like much of the TCI, the beach is fringed by a coral reef system with fabulous snorkeling and diving. See chapter 5.

- **Malcolm Beach** (Providenciales): The traditional way to see this charming cove (often referred to as Malcolm Roads Beach) is with a 4×4 along twisting, bumpy Malcolm Roads. You can also access the beach by staying at Amanyara (the resort is adjacent to the beach) or by getting a tour-boat operator to take you there. Its waters are part of the Northwest Point Marine National Park. See chapter 5.

- **Long Bay** (Providenciales): The calm, shallow waters of this quiet beach on Provo's southeastern shore make it perfect for young children. Take a horseback ride on the beach here with Provo Ponies. See chapter 5.

- **Sapodilla Bay and Taylor Bay** (Providenciales): Part of the Chalk Sound National Park, these shallow bays along Provo's southwest coastline have soft, silty bottoms and stunning blue water. See chapter 5.

- **Pine Cay** (Caicos Cays): The money shot in many a photo spread of Caribbean islands is often this private island's perfect crescent of sand, ringed by azure seas. It's the front yard of the Meridian Club resort. See chapters 3 and 5.

- **Parrot Cay** (Caicos Cays): Another gorgeous private island, this one with a secluded beach graced by beach bums of the celebrity variety. See chapters 3 and 5.

- **Sandy Point** (North Caicos): Up until now, only boaters and those in the know found their way to this spectacular beach, within sight of the Parrot Cay Resort. See chapter 5.

Best Beaches in the Turks & Caicos Islands

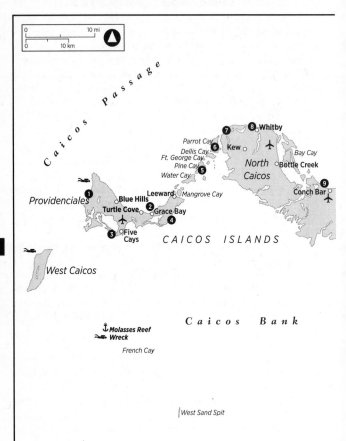

Bambarra Beach **10**
The beaches of Salt Cay **13**
Governor's Beach **12**
Grace Bay **2**
Long Bay **4**
Malcolm Beach **1**
Mudjin Harbor **9**
Parrot Cay **6**
Pillory Beach **11**
Pine Cay **5**
Sandy Point **7**
Sapodilla Bay & Taylor Bay **3**
Whitby beaches **8**

ATLANTIC

OCEAN

Middle Caicos

⑩ Bambarra
Lorimers

East Caicos

South Caicos

Cockburn Harbour
Six Hill Cays
Long Cay

Fish Cay

Big Ambergris Cay
Little Ambergris Cay

Seal Cays   Bush Cay

Turks Islands Passage

Grand Turk

⑪ Cockburn Town

TURKS ISLANDS

⑫ Long Cay

Cotton Cay
East Cay

Balfour Town ⑬ Salt Cay

Mouchoir Passage

Big Sand Cay

⚓ HMS Endymion Wreck

- **Whitby beaches** (North Caicos): The coves of **Three Mary Cays** are prime snorkeling spots. Step into the shallows of the palm-fringed **Pelican Point Beach** (in front of Pelican Beach Hotel) and find conch shells of every size. Lovely **Horsestable Beach** has enjoyed its North Caicos seclusion for years (it's also a prime bird-watching spot). See chapter 5.

- **Mudjin Harbor** (Middle Caicos): This beach is as stunning seen from the limestone cliffs towering above as it is up close. You can explore the wind-swept coves and snorkel in the turquoise shallows below. See chapter 5.

- **Bambarra Beach** (Middle Caicos): Casuarina trees fringe this picturesque, untrammeled beach. Its shallow aquamarine waters are the site of the festive Valentine's Day model sailboat races, and the Middle Caicos Day beach party is held here in August. See chapter 5.

- **Governor's Beach** (Grand Turk): Grand Turk's most celebrated beach has great snorkeling and is a popular picnic spot under shady pines. It's in the Columbus Landfall National Park—more about Columbus's "landfall" later—and within sightlines of the Grand Turk Cruise Center, which welcomes mammoth cruise ships 4 to 6 days a week. See chapter 6.

- **Pillory Beach** (Grand Turk): The Bohio Dive Resort is set on this handsome stretch of Grand Turk beach. See chapter 6.

- **The beaches of Salt Cay:** This tiny island has some of the best snorkeling beaches in the Caribbean. The best slices of sand may be found on North Beach and Point Pleasant. See chapter 6.

2 THE BEST OUTDOOR ADVENTURES

The waters here are superlative for all kinds of outdoor adventures, from diving and snorkeling to sailing, kayaking, and fishing. But watersports aren't the only game in town. You'll find prime golf and tennis facilities in Provo—and Rollerblade hockey is all the rage with local school kids. See chapters 5 and 6 for more on outdoor sports.

- **Snorkeling the islands:** The snorkeling opportunities are excellent throughout the islands, whether the Caicos Cays, North Caicos, Middle Caicos, South Caicos, Grand Turk, or Salt Cay. But you don't even have to leave Grace Bay to find good snorkeling. The government has established snorkel trails at Smith's Reef (just outside Turtle Cove) and Bight Reef (right in front of the Coral Gardens resort). These reefs are right off the shoreline, providing easy access to a fragile but beautiful world. See chapter 5.

- **Taking a beach cruise** (Caicos Cays): A number of tour-boat operators offer variations on half- and full-day beach sojourns. Your trip may include a stop on **Little Water Cay,** a protected nature reserve inhabited by a colony of rare rock iguanas; snorkeling the coral reefs and diving for conch; or combing the beaches of uninhabited cays for sand dollars and other shells. See the "Caicos Watersports Operators: Master List" box on p. 106.

- **Riding horses on the beach** (Long Bay, Provo): You don't need a whit of riding experience to thoroughly enjoy a leisurely late-afternoon trot on a beautiful beach. The gentle mounts of Provo Ponies are perfect for novices, but they don't mind kicking it up a bit for proven riders—they love a good beach gallop, too. See chapter 5.

- **Strolling Grace Bay before sunset:** You'll be surprised at the long stretches of beautiful beach you have all to yourself. The sand is a little cooler, and the water takes on the pink and purple hues of the setting sun. Stop in and sink into an inviting white-cushioned perch at the **Lounge** (p. 123) or the **Infinity Bar** (p. 123), the oceanfront bars at the Grace Bay Club, and sip a cocktail while you wait for the green flash on the horizon during sunset (seeing it is said to bring good luck). See chapter 5.

- **Watching the glowworms glow:** Four or five days after a full moon, millions of glowworms come out just after sunset to mate—lighting up the shallow waters with a sparkling green glow. Take a glowworm cruise in the Caicos Cays or off any number of Caicos Bank docks. The show is over when the mating ritual ends and the female glowworms devour the males. See chapter 5.

- **Hiking or biking the Crossing Place Trail** (Middle Caicos): This old coastal road, first established in the late 1700s by settlers and slaves working the local plantations, has been reopened from the Conch Bar to the Indian Cave field-road section and is now a National Trust heritage site. It has heartbreakingly beautiful sections, some on bluffs overlooking the blue-green ocean shallows and rocky outcrops; others bordered by island brush that includes wild sea-island cotton, remnants of the 18th-century plantations, and elegant sisal plants. Follow hiking or biking trails; when you get hot, take a swim in the shallow coves below. Be sure to visit **Conch Bar Cave,** a massive aboveground limestone cave system used by Lucayan Indians some 600 years ago. See chapter 5.

- **Diving the Wall off Grand Turk:** You can find great scuba-diving spots throughout the TCI, including spectacular opportunities off Provo's Northwest Point and in West Caicos. But Grand Turk's electrifying dives are just some 274m (900 ft.) offshore, where the continental shelf drops off from the coral reef in dramatic fashion. Along the ledges of this sheer wall is marine life in all its eye-popping plumage. See p. 136.

- **Whale-Watching on Salt Cay:** From January through April, humpback whales migrate along the 7,000-foot trench of the Columbus Passage (which snakes between the Turks islands and the Caicos islands) to the Silver Banks to mate and calf. You can actually snorkel and swim alongside these gentle 15m (50-ft.) creatures. See chapter 6.

- **Finding treasures on the beach:** The currents drop off a good amount of flotsam on these windward TCI beaches—much of it worthless junk. But hey, one man's trash is another man's inspiration. Nearly every island has a visionary artist or two who dabbles in beach salvage. Of course, real treasures do wash up: In 2006, silver pieces of eight and an 18th-century spyglass were picked up on the Salt Cay beaches. And bottles containing messages have found their way here from all over the world; the Turks & Caicos National Museum has a collection of messages in a bottle. The water's edge also yields gorgeous shells, from snow-white sand dollars to queen conch shells—but remember: Always return a shell back into the sea if something is living inside. See chapters 5 and 6.

3 FROMMER'S FAVORITE LUXURY RESORTS

Most of the country's accommodations are on Providenciales, where condo hotels are the prevailing lodging option.

- **Amanyara,** Northwest Point, Provo (© **866/941-8133**): The Singapore-based Amanresorts' first foray into the West Indies, which deftly marries pampered luxury with an exacting Eastern aesthetic; the name means "peaceful place." The guest pavilions are utterly private and smartly appointed in Aman teakwood, polished terrazzo floors, and state-of-the-art toys for grownups. See p. 76.

- **The Gansevoort,** Grace Bay, Provo (© **888/844-5986**): Urban escapees are making a beeline for this great-looking new Lower Bight property; it's definitely in their comfort zone. It's got a happening pool scene, a sizzling restaurant, and ultrastylish rooms with irresistible touches, like electric blinds, big freestanding tubs (filled from a ceiling tap), and glass-encased rain showers. See p. 63.

- **Grace Bay Club,** Grace Bay, Provo (© **800/946-5757**): This Grace Bay pioneer continues to reinvent itself, and everything, from the spacious luxury suites to the unparalleled service, is first-rate. Don't expect attitude, however; this is one of the warmest, most welcoming spots in town. You can even have a private dinner served under the stars on the beach. See p. 64.

- **Point Grace,** Grace Bay, Provo (© **866/924-7223**): Set on a stunning bend of Grace Bay beachfront, this resort gets consistent high marks for its handsomely appointed British-Colonial–style suites and ultraromantic restaurant, Grace's Cottage, one of Provo's top places to dine. See p. 65.

- **The Regent Palms,** Grace Bay, Provo (© **866/877-7256**): There are no bad rooms at this gorgeous resort, with a serpentine infinity pool, shops, restaurants, and a 25,000-square-foot spa with reflecting pools. It offers both serenity and a lively nightlife, with the Plunge Bar heating up at sunset. See p. 66.

- **The Somerset,** Grace Bay, Provo (© **877/887-5722**): Size matters, and this Tuscan-style boutique resort is just small enough to have a personalized, intimate feel and big enough to offer sprawling luxury suites with monumental balconies and marble-clad kitchens and baths. It has a sunny, serene atmosphere and a beautifully landscaped pool and beachfront. The house restaurant, O'Soleil, is one of Provo's best. See p. 67.

- **The Veranda,** Grace Bay, Provo (© **877/945-5757**): It looks like Main Street by the Sea, more like a movie-set village than an upscale resort: houses with gingerbread trim, picket fences, rockers on wooden porches, and broad swathes of neatly trimmed green. Once this new oceanfront resort is fully operational, it will have kid-specific areas with lots of fun stuff for the little ones. See p. 68.

- **West Bay Club,** Grace Bay, Provo (© **866/607-4156**): This new boutique oceanfront property has 46 spacious, beautifully appointed suites with full kitchens and marble-clad bathrooms. But unlike its neighbor the Gansevoort, West Bay has no hipster lounge or state-of-the-art spa. In fact, the pool is small, the modest restaurant has only nine tables, and the bar is just a smattering of stools. Everything but the spacious accommodations has been scaled down, and that's purely by design: Here it's all about those rooms and that beach and a warm and welcoming hands-on management that makes you feel as if you're old pals. Call it mom-and-pop luxe. See p. 72.

- **Parrot Cay Resort,** Parrot Cay, Provo (© **866/388-0036**): Yes, this is the exclusive island resort where Ben Affleck married Jennifer Garner and Bruce Willis owns a home. But it's also a pretty wonderful place to unwind and de-stress, whether you're stretched out on the secluded beach or thrilling to a treatment by a Balinese masseuse at the world-class COMO Shambhala spa. See p. 78.

- **The Meridian Club,** Pine Cay, Provo (© 866/746-3229): This is luxury of a determinedly downscale variety. You won't have TV, phones, radios, even air-conditioning, but you'll want for little else on this secluded private island, which offers the kind of solitude and serenity found in few places in the world. The beach and watersports opportunities are superb. See p. 79.
- **Grand Turk Inn,** Front Street, Grand Turk (©/fax 649/946-2827): The big, comfortable suites are laid-back luxury personified. The innkeepers, sisters who've lived all over the world, are hospitality pros, and their loving restoration of the 150-year-old Methodist manse has created Grand Turk's best accommodations. See p. 131.

4 THE BEST MODERATELY PRICED LODGINGS

Let's face it: Bargain hotel rooms in Provo are few and far between (you can still find affordable lodging on the other islands, however). Keep in mind that one way to save on hotel rates is by taking advantage of the special packages advertised on most hotel websites, offering decreased rates and extra perks with extended stays. You can also find hotel (and hotel/air) packages on popular travel-booking websites like Expedia and Travelocity, particularly in the off-season (mid-Apr to Nov). And don't forget to look into villa rentals (see chapter 2 for more information). Here are my choices for the best of the islands' less-expensive accommodations.

- **Sibonné Beach Hotel,** Grace Bay, Provo (© 800/528-1905): A stay here means a room just steps away from the waters of Grace Bay for a steal. Small and charming Sibonné is one of the oldest resorts on Grace Bay, and its rooms—all of which have sea views, by the way—are nothin' fancy but nicely appointed. But the real steal is the oceanfront apartment with full kitchen and two patios—one screened and one open, each with the same meltingly lovely view of Grace Bay that many of its pricier neighbors share. See p. 75.
- **Caribbean Paradise Inn,** Grace Bay, Provo (© 877/946-5020): The owner, Jean Luc Bohic, has fashioned a comfy little B&B around a tropical courtyard and pool, a 2-minute stroll from Grace Bay. The gourmet restaurant Coyaba moved here in 2006, bringing in a lively scene at night. See p. 74.
- **Comfort Suites,** Grace Bay, Provo (© 888/678-3483): This is a perfectly decent place to stay; the pool area is attractive, and the

suites are spacious. And the location is prime: 1 block from Grace Bay and next door to the Ports of Call shops. See p. 75.

- **Pelican Beach Hotel,** Pelican Beach, North Caicos (© 649/946-7112): The price is right at this small, comfortable spot smack-dab on Pelican Point. Rooms are admittedly nothing special, but the beach is grand—and the food, cooked by owner Susie Gardiner, is superb home-style island fare. See p. 81.
- **Blue Horizon Resort,** Mudjin Harbor, Middle Caicos (© 649/946-6141): New owners have spruced things up here, though don't expect the hermetic seal of a luxury, air-chilled Provo suite. Do expect, however, a comfy perch over some of the most breathtaking views on the islands, a world-class beach at your feet, and the sense of having a stretch of paradise largely to yourself ('cause it won't be so for long). See p. 81.
- **Osprey Beach Hotel,** Duke Street, Grand Turk (© 649/946-2666): You're in the thick of the Duke Street action, yet just steps away from the solitude of the island's southwestern beach. Many of the rooms have four-poster beds and cool white linens, and all are large and clean; those in the main section have private oceanfront patios. You'll see lots of familiar faces from all over the island at the barbecue around the pool every Sunday and Wednesday night. See p. 133.
- **Island House,** Lighthouse Road, Grand Turk (© 649/946-1519): The late British-born owner, Colin Brooker, was charm personified, and his small inn exemplified gracious island hospitality. Perched on a Grand Turk hill, the newly renovated inn has killer views of the sea and the island's sloping green bluffs. The freshwater pool is set in a lovely courtyard framed in tropical vegetation. You aren't on the beach, but the inn provides all guests with a vehicle to get around the island. See p. 131.
- **Bohio Dive Resort,** Front Street, Grand Turk (© 649/946-2135): Set in a prime location on beautiful Pillory Beach, this hotel has rebuilt after Hurricane Ike, and its rooms (the suites have kitchenettes) are spacious and clean; ask about the reasonable dive/lodging packages. Bohio has a good restaurant and a bar overlooking the beach. See p. 130.

5 FROMMER'S TOP FAMILY RESORTS

The TCI is as much a first-rate family destination as it is a top honeymoon retreat. Plenty of properties offer ways to entertain and pamper the kids. Here are my top choices for great family fun.

- **Beaches Turks & Caicos,** Lower Bight Road, Provo (© **800/232-2437**): Beaches keeps walking away with top honors as one of the region's top family resorts. And why not? It's got Sesame Street characters ambling around the property, camps and daily activities, kid-targeted restaurants, and a full-service nursery. And somehow the landscaping is kept immaculate. See p. 58.
- **Grace Bay Club,** Grace Bay, Provo (© **800/946-5757**): The setup here couldn't be better for accommodating both families and romantic twosomes—each has its own set of villas, pools, and restaurants. The resort's Kids' Town has a clubhouse with daily activities and "campouts" on the beach. See p. 64.
- **Ocean Club Resorts,** Grace Bay, Provo (© **800/457-8787**): It's family fun all the time at these popular resorts, with day camps, great pools, and kitchens. See p. 69.
- **Royal West Indies,** Grace Bay, Provo (© **800/332-4203**): This sprawling resort is another spot that deftly accommodates both families and couples, with full kitchen facilities and a great kiddie pool set apart from the "Quiet Zone" pool. It's got a terrific casual restaurant that somehow satisfies both grownups and little ones. See p. 71.
- **The Sands at Grace Bay,** Grace Bay, Provo (© **877/777-2637**): This has always been one of the top spots in Provo for families (fully equipped kitchens, nice pool, great beach), and with a major makeover and refurbishment, it's better than ever. It even has a giant toy box in the sands of Grace Bay crammed with beach toys. See p. 71.
- **Seven Stars,** Grace Bay, Provo (© **866/570-7777**): With a big kids' playground and lockout capacity for 2- and 3-bedroom suites, this resort is tailor-made for families. It's got the only heated pool on the island (saltwater, too!), a nice touch for little ones learning to swim. See p. 66.
- **The Somerset,** Grace Bay, Provo (© **877/887-5722**): Its sprawling suites are tailor-made for families, as is the infinity pool. Add to that a kid-friendly Caribbean staff that gets to know the little ones on a first-name basis, a big enticement for families to come back year after year. See p. 67.
- **West Bay Club,** Grace Bay, Provo (© **866/607-4156**): The nicely appointed suites have full kitchens, roomy bathrooms, and enormous closet space. The pool has a tiered section for toddlers, and the hands-on management couldn't be more hospitable. Plus you're just 10 minutes away in either direction from good beachfront snorkeling. See p. 72.
- **The Veranda,** Grace Bay, Provo (© **877/945-5757**): It looks like Main Street by the Sea, a movie-set village with gingerbread trim,

rockers on wooden porches, and broad swathes of neatly trimmed green. Once this new oceanfront resort is fully operational, it will have kid-specific areas with lots of fun stuff for the little ones. See p. 68.

6 FROMMER'S FAVORITE DINING EXPERIENCES

You will eat very well indeed on these islands, whether dining on fresh conch in an outdoor beach shack or sampling a chef's multicourse tasting menu in an elegant five-star resort. Here are some top picks.

- **Anacaona,** Grace Bay, Provo (© **649/946-5050**): The setting for the Grace Bay Club's premier restaurant is unbeatable: You're seated under the stars, surrounded by flaming torches, on a tiered and lushly planted landing overlooking Grace Bay Beach. The food can be as dreamy as the ambience. See p. 88.

- **Bagatelle Bistrot,** Grace Bay, Provo (© **649/946-5746**): This urbane spot takes service on the TCI to a whole other level, with serious food and a sophisticated wine list in a sleek indoor/outdoor space dotted with towering palm trees. It's downtown NYC meets cosmopolitan South Beach—but the breezy vibe is all Provo. See p. 89.

- **Baci Ristorante,** Turtle Cove, Harbour Towne, Provo (© **649/ 941-3044**): This Italian restaurant has a fabulous setting on the docks of the Turtle Cove marina. Lacy iron doors lead out to terraced outdoor seating on the water. The food is standard Italian— fettuccine Alfredo, lasagne alla Bolognese—but hearty and good, and relief from all that conch. See p. 96.

- **Bay Bistro,** Sibonné Beach Hotel, Grace Bay, Provo (© **649/946-5396**): It's one of the most pleasant spots to dine in Provo—set in a whitewashed wooden open-air porch above Grace Bay beach. The food is quite good and good value for Grace Bay. See p. 93.

- **Coco Bistro,** Grace Bay, Provo (© **649/946-5369**): Most everyone who eats here comes away happy. It's both a special-occasion place (with a romantic setting) and a foodie haven. Owner/Executive Chef Stuart Gray is a hardworking, hands-on guy—you'll see him hollering out food orders as the glitterati swoop in. See p. 90.

- **Da Conch Shack,** Blue Hills, Provo (© **649/946-8877**): Like many of its Blue Hills compadres, Da Conch Shack has a great setting (outdoors overlooking the beach), good, fresh food (conch pulled out of its shell on the beach below and prepared to order), and a laid-back, barefoot vibe. See p. 84.

- **Grace's Cottage,** Point Grace Hotel, Grace Bay (© **649/946-5096**): You'll see plenty of couples holding hands on these candlelit cottage patios (located outdoors and pillowed in tropical vegetation)—but when the grub arrives, it's every man for himself. See p. 91.
- **Magnolia Restaurant & Wine Bar,** Turtle Cove, Provo (© **649/941-5108**): The view alone is worth the trek up the hill above Turtle Cove marina, but the food easily stands on its own. Seared rare tuna is a house specialty. Have a drink and watch Grace Bay glitter. See p. 97.
- **Mango Reef,** Royal West Indies Resort, Grace Bay, Provo (© **649/946-8200**): It's not on the beach (it overlooks one of the resort's pools), and it's certainly not luxe. But this comfortable, casual spot is one of those places where the food is so consistently good you'll reach for excuses to eat here. Look around; you'll see locals, business folk, and other savvy diners chowing down. See p. 95.
- **Pat's Place,** Historic South District, Salt Cay (© **649/946-6919**): Pat taught school on Salt Cay for 28 years. She now serves home-style island cooking on a modest porch behind her home. You'll feel like Mom is behind the stove when she brings out her family-style platters of barbecued chicken, potato salad, and peas 'n' rice. See p. 145.

Planning Your Trip to the Turks & Caicos Islands

This chapter tackles the basics of a trip to the TCI, including everything from finding airfares to deciding whether to rent a car. But first, let's start with some background information about this island destination.

1 GETTING TO KNOW THE TURKS & CAICOS

It seems only yesterday that public awareness of this island archipelago was more or less "Turks and Caicos who?" For years, these islands were little more than a breathtakingly beautiful, slumbering backwater, home to a close-knit society of islanders called Belongers and the haunt of a smattering of fishermen and divers, beach bums and drug smugglers, and, of course, the well-heeled looking for an untouched cay in which to drop anchor.

Today the TCI is one of the premier destinations in the Caribbean, winning numerous travel industry accolades for its high-end, low-impact hospitality ethos. The action has largely concentrated on the main island, Providenciales ("Provo" for short), and its 19km (12-mile) beauty of a beach, Grace Bay. While many of the outlying islands retain the feel of an idyllic outpost, Provo has been on a dizzying growth spurt, becoming one of the fastest-growing spots in the Caribbean.

For a relatively new tourism destination, Provo has attracted an impressive lineup of world-class accommodations, a stable of resorts that few other rookie Caribbean destinations can claim. It's mind-boggling, really: Follow that long, sinuous stretch of Grace Bay beach and you'll pass such heavyweights as Club Med, the Regent Grand, Point Grace, the Somerset, the Regent Palms, and the Gansevoort. And just offshore is celebrity magnet Parrot Cay, the determinedly downscale luxury of the Meridian Club, and the Turks & Caicos Sporting Club (a Greenbrier affiliate) on Ambergris Cay.

A Fine Mess

The first 10 years of the 21st century have been tempestuous ones for the TCI: The islands were buffeted by hurricanes, a global recession, and a major government scandal. In 2009, the U.K. took the unprecedented steps of stripping this British colony of its powers of self-governance (forcing the high-living premier to resign in the process), suspending the constitution, and installing a British governor, at least for the next 2 years—measures taken after an official Commission of Inquiry found a "culture of corruption" at the highest levels of government. Court documents told of government ministers allegedly pocketing wads of cash in exchange for prime development deals and the granting of highly prized "Belongerships" (citizenship status). But the most riveting testimony revolved around the extravagant lifestyle of former premier Michael Misick, including his tempestuous marriage to a Hollywood star, their personal staff (which cost the TCI government some half-a-mil a year), and the marbled and pillared "White House" the couple built in Leeward—at press time for sale for $16 million. And the marriage between Misick and his former first lady—always impeccably turned out in her trademark white? *Finis.*

In fact, things were going swimmingly, with resorts ratcheting up the luxe factor, until the islands were hit with a triple whammy: the devastating hurricane of 2008, the global recession, and the country's own little constitutional crisis (see "A Fine Mess," below). In 2009, the boom came to a thudding halt. Projects stalled or went into receivership. Nikki Beach, the glitzy nightclub brand, shut down its resort in Leeward in 2009. Construction on the much-touted Ritz-Carlton project on West Caicos came to a stop, and plans to zap sweet little Salt Cay into a luxury golf resort were put on ice.

Today, the bones of unfinished resorts hover over pricey beachfronts. The Toscana, in the Lower Bight, looks like a burned-out Tara, its unfinished frame rising out of the sand amid a goofy stand of transplanted pine trees. The Royal Reef Resort, on Sandy Point in North Caicos, is a stark concrete pile within view of Parrot Cay's exclusive beaches. Perhaps the biggest thud heard 'round the islands was the demise of the much-ballyhooed resort on Dellis Cay, one of the Caicos Cays, where a handful of world-renowned "starchitects" was tapped to design a Mandarin Oriental hotel, villas, and homesites

A Little History

The earliest inhabitants of these islands were Lucayan Indians, who settled in the Bahamas archipelago some 800 years before Columbus arrived in the New World. Some historians believe that Grand Turk was the site of Columbus's first landfall—and experts have established that the explorer was indeed greeted on his arrival by Lucayan Indians—but no hard evidence exists to support this theory either way. The Lucayans' idyllic existence came to an end when Spanish explorers arrived, enslaving the natives and exposing them to diseases. In a generation, the Lucayan population was wiped out. Habitation was spotty after that, with the islands passing through Spanish, French, and British control and industries coming and going—from **salt-raking,** which drew Bermudans—and the British crown—in the late 17th century, to **cotton,** which brought Loyalists fleeing the States after the American Revolution. The cotton industry was eventually done in by storms and pests, and by the early 19th century, the main inhabitants left on the islands were the slaves that had been brought in to work the plantations. The salt industry—labor-intensive work that broke the backs of many a worker in the tropical heat—lasted until the 1960s, around the time a small airstrip was built on Provo and a nascent tourist industry began to stir. But it wasn't until 1984, when the development of Club Med led to the construction of a larger airport, that commercial tourism started to take root on the Turks and Caicos Islands.

starting at around $2 million (with celebrities like Michael Douglas and Catherine Zeta-Jones on board).

WHY THE TCI?

Why was little TCI ripe for all this tourism activity in the first place? For one, the country's beaches, water, and coral reef system remain astonishingly unspoiled. The seas have an intense blue-green hue that puts Technicolor to shame. The climate—best described as an "eternal summer"—is ideal year-round. Gentle breezes blow in from the east, instant relief from the relentless sun. For North Americans, the TCI has other pluses: English is the official language, the U.S. dollar is the local

Turks & Caicos at a Glance

Location: The Turks and Caicos archipelago is located in the British West Indies, 48km (30 miles) south of the Bahamas, 161km (100 miles) northeast of the Dominican Republic, and 925km (575 miles) southeast of Miami. The TCI is not officially in the Caribbean—it's in the Atlantic Ocean.

Population: The country's population is approximately 30,000 people. Citizens of the TCI, called "Belongers," are primarily the descendants of African slaves and comprise more than half the islands' population. A large group of Haitian expats live and work in the TCI (many of them so long they have become Belongers). Other expat groups include a growing number of Jamaicans and Filipinos.

Size: The two island groups—the Turks islands and the Caicos islands—together comprise 500 sq. km (193 sq. miles) and are separated by the 35km (22-mile) **Columbus Passage,** the sea route Christopher Columbus took during his exploration of the New World in 1492.

Economy: Tourism, fishing, and the offshore finance industry are the big three. Regarding the latter, the islands are a "zero tax" jurisdiction and have no taxes on income, capital gains, corporate profits, inheritance, or estates. There are no controls on transferring funds or assets in or out of the country.

Government: The TCI is a British Crown Colony. A queen-appointed governor holds executive power and presides over an Executive Council. A 1987 constitution established a representative democracy, and today the local government is elected by the citizens and includes a premier (the country's first), a deputy premier, other ministers, and a legislative council empowered to enact local statutes. The TCI seat of government is Cockburn Town in Grand Turk. *Note:* At press time, corruption concerns have led the British government to suspend the constitution and assume governance of the island for at least 2 years. The plan is to return self-rule to the island once governmental safeguards have been put into place.

Last time the queen visited: 1966. Elizabeth II stopped in at South Caicos for the day, sailing in on the royal yacht *Britannia.*

currency, and the islands are easily accessible by plane. Nonstop flights out of places like New York City (3 hr.), Boston (3½ hr.), Charlotte (2 hr.), and Miami (1½ hr.) mean you can jump on a plane in the morning and be lazing about on a tropical beach by early afternoon.

And until the economy went, well, south, the islands also enjoyed zero unemployment—although much of its work force is now drawn from off-island, from places like Haiti, Jamaica, and even the Philippines (the native TCI population is relatively small). Even more important, it has one of the lowest crime rates in the Caribbean. Yes, there is petty crime, but you simply do not see the kind of impoverishment and homelessness that continue to plague other Caribbean countries.

The island citizens—"the Belongers"—enjoy one of the best primary and secondary educational systems in the region. The Belongers share such a warm familiarity that it's easy to see why many have embraced the possibility that all are connected by blood, descended from the 193 African slaves freed on these isolated islands when the slave ship *Trouvadore,* carrying them to lives of bondage in the Americas, wrecked on the East Caicos reef in 1841. Research is underway by a Turks & Caicos National Museum expedition team to discern whether a shipwreck found off East Caicos in 2004 is the *Trouvadore*—and if so, whether its inhabitants were indeed the progenitors of the modern-day Belongers. For the latest information, go to www.tcmuseum.org/projects/slave-ship-trouvadore.

For those who knew and loved the TCI in slower times and who had concerns that the islands were in danger of being overdeveloped (or even ruinously developed), it's comforting to know that of the 40 islands that compose the TCI, only 10 are inhabited. Even the most populous beach, Provo's Grace Bay, has long, dreamy stretches where you're the only soul on the soft sand. The focus has been on sustainable development and low-impact, high-end properties—boutique resorts with ecologically sensitive bones—a vision held in large part through the fizzy boom times. And perhaps the financial recession/constitutional crisis is something of a blessing in disguise, a necessary stopgap for a runaway train. With things moving at a little slower pace, perhaps the business side will be more in tune with the natural rhythms of the island nation—essential for the survival of both. For the islanders who live and work in the TCI, and for travelers who love its bounteous beauty and soul, that's awfully heartening.

2 THE ISLANDS IN BRIEF

The TCI topography is pretty prosaic. The islands are low lying, with sandy soil and a low scrub cover, but each one has its own unique look and feel. North Caicos, the so-called garden island, is a sprawling rural landscape rimmed by blue-green seas. Middle Caicos has soft emerald cliffs overlooking rocky coves, beaches fringed by casuarina trees, and the occasional cotton or sisal plant left over from plantation days. Grand Turk, Salt Cay, and South Caicos are low-key charmers that hold quaint architectural remnants of the islands' colonial past, while much in Provo (Providenciales) is as bright and shiny as a new penny. All have stupendous soft-sand beaches lapped by tranquil azure seas.

In an interesting twist, the boom that hit Provo has drawn people to tourist-industry jobs away from their homes—and traditional livelihoods—on the other islands. In Middle Caicos in particular, you'll see homes abandoned to the underbrush, and once-thriving communities reduced nearly to ghost towns. To ensure that the traditional cultures and way of life on the islands aren't lost forever, the **Turks & Caicos National Trust** has made it its mission to "safeguard the natural, historical and cultural heritage of the Turks and Caicos Islands." To find out more about the National Trust's latest projects, go to the website www.nationaltrust.tc.

THE CAICOS ISLANDS

PROVIDENCIALES The 98-sq.-km (38-sq.-mile) island of **Providenciales (Provo)** and its splendid 19km (12-mile) Grace Bay beach were a tourist mecca waiting to happen. In the early 1980s, Club Med was the only game in town until the government opened the door to boutique resort development. Now Provo's tourist infrastructure far surpasses anything on Grand Turk, the TCI seat of government. This is where the action is, literally, with the bulk of the country's lodging, dining, tours, activities, and entertainment. Still, don't expect a bustling metropolis: Provo is a pretty laidback place to be—and that's a big part of its charm. One of the larger islands of the Turks and Caicos, Provo is largely flat and arid, with miles of scrubland. Today, Provo is the entry point and main destination for most visitors to the TCI.

CAICOS CAYS Also called the Leeward Cays, these gorgeous little islands were once the haven of pirates. Many are still uninhabited except by day-trippers beachcombing and snorkeling the shallows, while others are private islands with secluded resorts. Little Water Cay is a National Trust nature reserve and home to the endangered rock iguana.

NORTH CAICOS Former TCI Premier Michael Misick once called North Caicos, his birthplace, "a tiger awakening." The projected site of the second big TCI boom remains a sleepy rural landscape, however. Roads are much improved, and a deepwater harbor built to accommodate freight-bearing ships (and a ferry btw. North and

Provo) has been completed. But the beaches remain unspoiled and untrammeled, and lodgings and restaurants few and far between. Locals say this sparsely populated, 106-sq.-km (41-sq.-mile) island is a snapshot of Provo before the boom.

MIDDLE CAICOS The largest island in the Turks and Caicos (125 sq. km/48 sq. miles), Middle Caicos has a correspondingly small full-time population (300 people). It's a landscape of contrasts. Soft green slopes overlook beautiful Mudjin Harbor. Along the rise is Crossing Place Trail, a narrow 18th-century path so named because it leads to a place where people once crossed a sandbar at low tide to reach North Caicos. A massive aboveground limestone cave system used by Lucayan Indians some 600 years ago is here to be explored. At Bambarra Beach the sunlit aquamarine shallows stretch long into the horizon. Middle has little of Provo's tourism infrastructure; it attracts visitors who don't mind roughing it a bit amid a gorgeous seaside landscape. A causeway now links Middle to North Caicos—an essential link that is delivering more traffic to the island.

SOUTH CAICOS Hard hit by Hurricane Ike in 2008, this still-sleepy fishing community of some 1,200 people and 21 sq. km (8 sq. miles) is hearing faint rumblings of tourist development. Because the South Caicos tourist infrastructure is still in its infancy, this guide addresses the region only peripherally. But clearly, with its excellent diving and bonefishing opportunities and historic Bermudan-style architecture, "Big South" is an up-and-coming spot.

EAST CAICOS This unspoiled, uninhabited 47-sq.-km (18-sq.-mile) island was once for the home of large sisal and cotton plantations and the East Caicos Cattle Company. Now it's largely swampland and savanna and a few wild donkeys.

WEST CAICOS This lovely 29-sq.-km (11-sq.-mile) island (with a 202-hectare/500-acre nature preserve) is the site of some of the islands' best scuba diving. Still on hold at press time was a long-awaited five-star Ritz-Carlton resort, with the works: a 100-slip marina, villas, town houses, cottages, and a hotel.

THE TURKS ISLANDS

GRAND TURK People who only visit Provo miss out on experiencing the country's rich heritage. Enchanting Grand Turk, just 11×3km (7×2 miles), has colorful 19th-century Bermudian architecture, abandoned salinas where the business of salt-raking was conducted from the late 17th century until the 1960s, a 19th-century lighthouse, and a first-rate museum housed in the Guinep House, believed to be around 180 years old. Grand Turk is still recovering from the devastation brought by hurricanes Hanna and Ike in 2008. The small-town

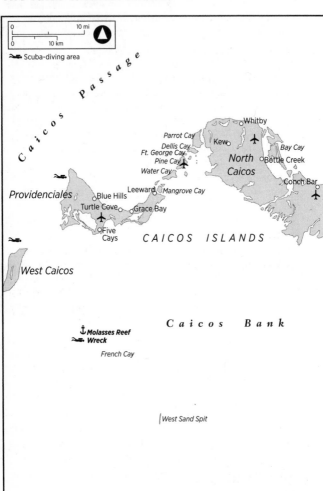

0 ____ 10 mi

0 ____ 10 km

Scuba-diving area

Caicos Passage

Parrot Cay
Dellis Cay
Ft. George Cay
Pine Cay
Water Cay

Whitby
Kew
Bay Cay
North Caicos Bottle Creek
Conch Bar

Leeward *Mangrove Cay*

Providenciales Blue Hills
Turtle Cove Grace Bay
Five Cays

CAICOS ISLANDS

West Caicos

Caicos Bank

⚓ *Molasses Reef Wreck*

French Cay

West Sand Spit

A T L A N T I C

O C E A N

atmosphere of Cockburn Town belies the fact that this Grand Turk village is the capital of the TCI. The diving here along the continental shelf wall is stupendous, traditionally the big draw for most visitors. That certainly was the case until 2006, when Carnival Cruise Lines opened a theme-park-style cruise terminal at the southwest end of the island to welcome the arrival of 2,000-passenger ships. Now a ship is in port 4 to 6 days a week. It's been a boon for local tour operators, taxi drivers, and entrepreneurs. (One casualty: the island's charming feral donkeys, which don't obey traffic signs or caravans of cruise-ship dune buggies. The donkeys are being shipped to the Dominican Republic, for their own safety, it's said.) Still, Grand Turk remains relatively undeveloped, with just a scattering of inns and restaurants. A new Conch Farm, a sister project to Provo's Conch Farm, has opened on the island's east coast. Among the uninhabited cays in the Grand Turk Cays Land and Sea National Park is Gibbs Cay, where you can swim in clear, shallow water with stingrays.

SALT CAY   Salt Cay (pop. 60) is the kind of place where you can paste salvaged flip-flops onto your neighbor's boat while he's away, and everyone (including your neighbor) thinks it's a hoot. It's the kind of place where a hermit crab race is the talk of the town. It's also the kind of place where people come from around the world to partake in world-class watersports activities (snorkeling, diving, whale-watching), swim in the luminescent green sea, and comb the secluded beaches for flotsam and jetsam. Salt Cay is admittedly small (6.5 sq. km/2½ sq. miles) and missing many of the basic accoutrements of 21st-century civilization (one ATM, just a handful of cars), but it is also the site of significant colonial-era buildings and at press time was under consideration for World Heritage Site status.

3 VISITOR INFORMATION

The **Turks and Caicos Tourist Board** (www.turksandcaicostourism. com) has offices in Stubbs Diamond Plaza, Providenciales (© **649/946-4970**), and Front Street, Cockburn Town, Grand Turk (© **649/946-2321**). The New York City office is now overseen by Pamela Ewing (© **646/375-8830**). In Canada, the tourist board has an office at 175 Bloor St. East, Ste. 307, South Tower, Toronto, ON (© **866/413-8875** or 416/642-9771).

SIGHTSEEING ON THE WEB   Whenever possible throughout this book, we've included Web addresses along with phone numbers and addresses for attractions, outfitters, and other companies. We've also given each hotel and resort's website, to give you a better idea of a property before you make your reservation. In addition, most hotels have special package deals only offered on their websites.

The following recommended Turks and Caicos–specific websites can be of enormous help in planning your trip:

- **www.turksandcaicos.tc**: The TCI Mall, sponsored by LIME, the television and Internet provider, is an exhaustive source of information. It's best in providing local community information (all the local newspapers are linked here) and provides a thorough rundown of each island (including the less-traveled islands).
- **http://turksandcaicoshta.com**: The official site of the Turks & Caicos Hotel and Tourism Association.
- **www.tcmuseum.org**: The Turks & Caicos National Museum is a delight. This website is an informative reflection of the museum's collection, the islands' history and culture, and the ongoing research projects affiliated with the museum.
- **www.nationaltrust.tc**: The site of the Turks & Caicos National Trust, a nonprofit, nongovernmental organization dedicated to the preservation of the cultural, historical, and natural heritage of the Turks and Caicos Islands.
- **www.timespub.tc**: The website for the *Times of the Islands,* a quarterly magazine that has meaty features on TCI flora and fauna, history, culture, food, and business.

4 WHEN TO GO

THE WEATHER

Aside from the idyllic seas and skies, the weather here is a big draw. The average temperature on the Turks and Caicos Islands ranges between 85° and 90°F (29°–32°C) from June to October, sometimes reaching the mid-90s (35°C), especially in the late summer months. From November to May the average temperature is 80° to 84°F (27°–29°C).

Water temperature in the summer is 82° to 84°F (28°–29°C) and in winter about 74° to 78°F (23°–26°C). A constant easterly trade wind keeps the climate at a very comfortable level.

Grand Turk and South Caicos have an annual rainfall of 53 centimeters (21 in.), but as you travel farther west, the average rainfall can increase to as much as 102 centimeters (40 in.). In an average year the Turks and Caicos Islands have 350 days of sunshine.

Mosquitoes and no-see-ums can be a problem year-round. However, more mosquitoes come out during the rainy season, which usually occurs in autumn.

If you come in the summer, be prepared for broiling sun in the midafternoon.

If you want to know how to pack just before you go, check the Weather Channel's online 10-day forecast at **www.weather.com** for the latest information.

Average Temperatures and Rainfall in Turks & Caicos

	Jan	Feb	Mar	Apr	May	June	July	Aug	Sept	Oct	Nov	Dec
Max (°F)	82	82	84	86	88	90	90	91	88	88	86	86
Max (°C)	28	28	29	30	31	32	32	33	31	31	30	30
Min (°F)	75	70	72	73	77	79	79	82	81	77	75	72
Min (°C)	21	21	22	23	25	26	26	28	27	25	24	22
Ave. rain (in.)	2	1.4	1.1	1.4	2.5	1.7	1.7	2	3.2	3.9	4.0	2.8

Source: Hutchinson World Weather Guide

HURRICANES The curse of Caribbean weather, the hurricane season lasts—officially, at least—from June 1 to November 30. But there's no cause for panic: Satellite forecasts give enough warning that precautions can be taken.

Until Hurricane Ike pummeled Grand Turk and South Caicos in 2008 (in the immediate wake of a drenching by Hurricane Hanna), the Turks and Caicos had been largely spared any serious hurricane havoc since 1960, when Hurricane Donna dropped 51 centimeters (20 in.) of rain in 24 hours (some say the mountains of Haiti and the Dominican Republic weaken hurricane-force winds before the storms reach the TCI). Still, hurricanes have wreaked havoc here in the past, including a September 1926 storm that brought 150-mph winds, slammed boulders on beaches, and had a storm surge that moved 1.2km (¾ mile) inland. And of course, Hurricane Ike in 2008 caused enormous destruction on Grand Turk—some 80% of the island's structures were damaged. Always monitor weather reports if you plan to visit during hurricane season. Check the **Weather Channel** on the Web at **www.weather.com**.

THE HIGH SEASON & THE OFF-SEASON

Like much of the Caribbean, the Turks and Caicos have become a year-round destination. The "season" runs roughly from mid-December to mid-April, which is generally the driest time of year in the Caribbean and the most miserable time of year in the northern U.S. and in Canada. Hotels charge their highest prices during the peak winter period, and you'll have to make your reservations well in advance—months in advance if you want to travel over the Christmas or New Year's holidays or in the depths of February, especially around Presidents' Day weekend. The Easter holidays/school spring break is an increasingly popular time for families to visit.

The off-season in the Turks and Caicos—roughly from mid-April to mid-November (although this varies from hotel to hotel)—is a perfectly nice time to come to the TCI: Yes, the temperatures are somewhat higher, but the southeasterly trade winds work to temper the heat, as do the brief but more frequent rain showers. The off-season is also one big sale. In most cases, hotels, inns, and condos slash 20% to 50% off their winter rates. Airfares are generally cheaper, and air/hotel packages can be very reasonable—even for stays at the top luxury lodgings. For many Europeans, who generally have longer vacation times, the summer is already a favorite time to visit the TCI.

Note: Some hotels use the off-season for refurbishment or bustling construction projects—which can be an annoyance if you're looking for peace and quiet. Make sure to ask what, if any, work is going on. If you decide to go anyway, ask for a room far away from the noise.

HOLIDAYS

New Year's Day (Jan 1); Commonwealth Day (observed on the Mon nearest Mar 12); Good Friday (celebrated the Fri prior to Easter); Easter Monday (celebrated on the Mon after Easter); National Heroes Day (observed the last Mon in May in honor of the First Chief Minister, the late Hon. J. A. G. S. McCartney); Queen's Official Birthday (observed mid-June); Emancipation Day (celebrated the first of Aug; this holiday commemorates the freedom of the slaves, which was declared from Oddfellows Lodge in Grand Turk in 1834); National Youth Day (celebrated the last Fri of Sept); Columbus Day (celebrated on the Mon nearest Oct 10; this holiday commemorates Christopher Columbus's "landing" on TCI in 1492—although no firm evidence exists to confirm that the explorer actually made a landfall here at all); International Human Rights Day (observed on Oct 24; this holiday is similar to the USA's July Fourth celebration); Christmas Day (Dec 25); Boxing Day (Dec 26; on this day the annual Church Fair takes place in the Grand Turk Methodist Church).

TURKS & CAICOS CALENDAR OF EVENTS

JANUARY

Junkanoo, island-wide. Junkanoo is held throughout the year for public holidays and local events, but the biggest Junkanoo celebrations are on Emancipation Day, Boxing Day, and the early morning of New Year's Day. Groups compete against each other for the most outrageous costumes, the best drummers, the best rhythm section, and more. Midnight to sunrise, New Year's Day morning.

FEBRUARY

Valentine's Day Cup, Bambarra Beach, Middle Caicos. Traditional Model Sailboat Race, with trophies and other prizes, is followed by music, dancing, food, and other festivities on the beach. The model sailboats are built in Bambarra from branches of the gum-elemi tree, constructed to scale with the actual rigging found on a full-size sloop. For more information, contact (C) **649/941-7639** or **middle caicos@tciway.tc.** Saturday closest to Valentine's Day.

MARCH

St. Patrick's Day Pub Crawl, Providenciales. Now in its 20th year, the crawl generally starts at the Tiki Hut and ends up at Danny Buoy's, with lots of suds along the way. Contact (C) **649/231-1645.** March 17.

APRIL

Annual Kite-Flying Competition, the Children's Park, Lower Bight Road, Providenciales. The 20th Annual Kite-Flying Competition in 2010 featured awards for best homemade kites, a beach party, an Easter egg hunt, and food and music. Contact (C) **649/ 946-4970.** Easter Monday.

MAY

Big South Regatta, South Caicos. The Big South Regatta, a tradition since 1967, features boat races, concerts, food, and entertainers. Contact (C) **649/946-4970.** Last weekend in May.

JUNE

Fools' Regatta, Providenciales. This beach party celebrating all things maritime features native sloops in sailing races and a sand-castle competition. The regatta is held to raise funds for local causes. Held at the Children's Park in the Bight. For details, go to http://maritimeheritage.tc. Mid-June.

Grand Turk Heineken Game Fishing Tournament, Grand Turk. Fish tourney at Governor's Beach features big cash prizes, music, barbecue, volleyball, and, of course, dominoes. For more information, call the Turks & Caicos Tourist Board at (C) **649/946-2321.** June 23 through June 25.

JULY

Turks & Caicos Music and Cultural Festival, Providenciales. This 8-day affair attracts big-name talent; the 2008 festival featured Lionel Ritchie and LL Cool J, among other musicians, and performances were aired on BET. It also features pageants, parades, and regattas. For more information, go to **www.musicfestival.tc** or call (C) **649/946-4970.** July 31 through August 7.

Emancipation Day, island-wide. Celebrating the freeing of the slaves, declared from Oddfellows Lodge in Grand Turk in 1834. August 1.

Middle Caicos Day, Middle Caicos. Parades, beauty pageants, music, food, bonfires, straw-weaving competitions, and an all-day beach party at Bambarra Beach. Contact ✆ **649/941-7639** or **middlecaicos@tciway.tc.** Last weekend in August.

SEPTEMBER

National Youth Day, island-wide. This public holiday celebrates the youth of the island. September 29.

OCTOBER

TCI Amateur Open, Providenciales. PricewaterhouseCoopers Limited sponsors this 3-day, 36-hole championship for both men and women, now in its 14th year, at the Provo Golf & Country Club. For more information, go to **www.provogolfclub.com.** Early October.

Columbus Day, island-wide. This public holiday celebrates Columbus's "discovery" of the New World. Some historians believe that the explorer first came ashore at Grand Turk. October 9.

NOVEMBER

Museum Day, Grand Turk. The Turks & Caicos National Museum celebrates the anniversary of its opening with loads of activities, including song and dance performances by local schoolchildren. For more information, go to **www.tcmuseum.org** or call ✆ **649/ 946-2160.** Saturday closest to November 21 (the day the museum opened in 1991).

Turks & Caicos Restaurant Week, Providenciales. This newly launched event will see participating restaurants offering three-course prix-fixe menus. For details, contact the Turks & Caicos Hotel and Tourism Association (TCHTA) at ✆ **649/941-5787** or www.turksandcaicoshta.com. First week in November.

Turks & Caicos Conch Festival, Providenciales. This is becoming the islands' premier event, and the conch-etition gets fiercer every year as local restaurants vie to win top honors for best conch concoctions, including conch chowder, conch curry, and conch salad. Now in its sixth year, the conch festival is a popular celebration, with music, food, conch-blowing, and a great seaside Blue Hills location. For more information, call ✆ **649/331-6832** or go to **www.conchfestival.com.** Last Saturday in November.

Christmas Tree-Lighting Ceremony, Providenciales. The Providenciales Kiwanis Club invites the public to the Downtown Ball Park for Christmas festivities, including a choir and a visit from Santa Claus. Mid-December.

Island Thyme Annual Xmas Tree Ornament Competition, Salt Cay. The best handmade ornaments are judged (and prizes given) at this popular and always festive restaurant. For more information, call ✆ **649/946-6977.** Call for exact date.

Old Year's Night, island-wide. Services at churches all over the country ring out the old and ring in the new. December 31.

5 ENTRY REQUIREMENTS

PASSPORTS

U.S. and Canadian citizens must have a passport or a combination of a birth certificate and photo ID, plus a return or ongoing ticket, to enter the country. Citizens of the United Kingdom, Commonwealth countries of the Caribbean, the Republic of Ireland, and E.U. countries must also have a current passport.

All travelers coming from the Caribbean, including Americans, are now required to have a passport to enter or reenter the United States. Those returning to Canada are also required to show passports. Cruise ship passengers must also meet the requirement. You'll certainly need identification at some point, and a passport is the best form of ID for speeding through Customs and Immigration. Driver's licenses are not acceptable as a sole form of ID.

CUSTOMS

Generally, you're permitted to bring in items intended for your personal use, including tobacco, cameras, film, and a limited supply of liquor—usually 40 ounces.

Just before you leave home, check with the Turks and Caicos Customs or Foreign Affairs department for the latest guidelines—including information on items that are not allowed to be brought into your home country—since the rules are subject to change and often contain some surprising oddities.

On arriving in the Turks and Caicos, you may bring in 1 quart of liquor, 200 cigarettes, 50 cigars, or 8 ounces of tobacco duty-free. There are no restrictions on cameras, film, sports equipment, or personal items, provided they aren't for resale. Absolutely no spear guns or Hawaiian slings are allowed, and the importation of firearms without a permit is also prohibited. Illegal imported drugs bring heavy fines and lengthy terms of imprisonment.

You should collect receipts for all purchases made abroad. You must also declare on your Customs form the nature and value of all gifts received during your stay abroad. It's prudent to carry proof that you purchased expensive cameras or jewelry on the U.S. mainland. If you purchased such an item during an earlier trip abroad, you should carry proof that you have previously paid Customs duty on the item.

Sometimes merchants suggest a false receipt to undervalue your purchase. *Beware:* You could be involved in a sting operation—the merchant might be an informer to U.S. Customs.

If you use any medication that contains controlled substances or requires injection, carry an original prescription or note from your doctor.

For specifics on what you can bring back, download the invaluable free pamphlet *Know Before You Go* online at www.cbp.gov. (Click on "Travel," then go to "Travel Smart" and click on "Know Before You Go.") Or contact the **U.S. Customs and Border Protection (CBP),** 1300 Pennsylvania Ave. NW, Washington, DC 20229 (© **877/287-8667**), and request the pamphlet.

U.K. citizens should contact **HM Customs & Excise** at © **0845/010-9000** (© 020/8929-0152 from outside the U.K.), or consult its website at www.hmce.gov.uk.

For a clear summary of **Canadian** rules, write for the booklet *I Declare,* issued by the **Canada Border Services Agency** (© **800/461-9999** in Canada, or 204/983-3500; www.cbsa-asfc.gc.ca).

Citizens of **Australia** should request a helpful brochure available from Australian consulates or Customs offices called *Know Before You Go.* For more information, call the **Australian Customs Service** at © **1300/363-263,** or log on to www.customs.gov.au.

For **New Zealand** Customs information, contact **New Zealand Customs** at © **04/473-6099** or 0800/428-786, or log on to www.customs.govt.nz.

6 GETTING THERE & GETTING AROUND

GETTING TO THE TURKS & CAICOS

The main point of entry for international flights into the Turks and Caicos is **Providenciales International Airport** (www.provoairport.com); Grand Turk and South Caicos also have international airports.

> **(Tips)   Never on a Sunday (or a Saturday)**
>
> If you can possibly swing it, avoid flying in or out of Provo on
> Saturday or Sunday during peak season. These are the days
> when the weekly villa or condo rentals turn over, and the
> modest-size airport is overrun with travelers arriving and
> departing—the result being that the Customs process at arriv-
> als can be agonizingly slow and the departure lines long and
> full of (understandably) cranky kids.

Underway at press time was a major upgrade for the Provo airport to
handle its growing influx of visitors—good news for fliers, since a
bigger airport means more competition and, hopefully, more competitive rates. (Where are you, JetBlue?) **American Airlines** (© 800/
433-7300 in the U.S. and Canada; www.aa.com) flies regular nonstop flights from New York, Boston, and Miami. Other airlines serving the islands include **Air Canada** (© 888/247-2262 in the U.S.
and Canada; www.aircanada.ca), which has direct flights from
Toronto, Montreal, and Ottawa; **WestJet** (© 888/937-8538; www.
westjet.com), flies twice weekly from Montreal and Toronto; **Bahamas Air** (© 800/222-4262; http://up.bahamasair.com) flies three
times weekly from Nassau; **British Airways** (© 800/247-9297 in the
U.S., 0870/850-9850 in the U.K.; www.britishairways.com), which
flies nonstop from London on Sunday; **Delta** (© 800/241-4141 in
the U.S. and Canada; www.delta.com), which flies nonstop daily
from Atlanta; and **US Airways** (© 800/622-1015 in the U.S. and
Canada; www.usairways.com), which flies nonstop from Charlotte
(daily), Boston, and Philadelphia. **Air Turks & Caicos** (© 649/946-
4181; www.airturksandcaicos.com) has regular flights between Provo
and Jamaica, Haiti, the Dominican Republic, and the Bahamas.

The Provo airport is small, with limited tourist services. A restaurant, **Gilley's Cafe** (© 649/946-4472; open 7 days a week for breakfast and lunch), is near the domestic arrivals and departures area—it
has surprisingly good food and a dynamite (good *and* spicy) conch
chowder. The international departure lounge has a few duty-free
shops—including **Jai's** (© 649/941-4324), which sells fine jewelry;
Maison Creole (© 649/946-4748), which sells charming hand-
crafted items (most of which are made in Haiti); and **Turquoise
Duty-Free** (© 649/946-4536), which sells liquor and Cuban and
Dominican cigars—but the only food source is a snack bar with
microwave pizza, chips, gum, and drinks. If you have a long wait

---

(Tips) Getting Through the Airport

- Arrive at the airport 1 hour before a domestic flight and 2 hours before an international flight; if you show up late, locate an airline employee and he or she will probably whisk you to the front of the line.
- Beat the ticket-counter lines by using airport electronic kiosks or even online check-in from your home computer, from where you can print out boarding passes in advance. Curbside check-in is also a good way to avoid lines (although if you have luggage to check, keep in mind that most curbside check-ins now charge fees to check baggage).
- Bring a passport. Children 17 and under are also now required to have passports to enter or reenter the U.S.
- Speed up security by removing your jacket and shoes before you're screened. In addition, remove metal objects such as big belt buckles. If you've got metallic body parts, a note from your doctor can prevent a long chat with the security screeners.
- Use a TSA-approved lock for your checked luggage. Look for Travel Sentry certified locks at luggage or travel shops.
- Follow **Transportation Security Administration (TSA)** regulations when packing your carry-on luggage. Follow the agency's "3-1-1" policy, which limits the volume of liquids, gels, and aerosols to bottles 3 ounces or smaller (or 100 ml), in 1 quart-size zip-top bag, and 1 bag per traveler. Log on to **www.tsa.gov/travelers/index.shtm** for details.

---

ahead of you—and hungry kids in tow—consider getting a bite at Gilley's before your flight.

Flying for Less: Tips for Getting the Best Airfare

You can often save money by buying your airfare as part of a vacation package. In most cases, a package to the Turks and Caicos will include airfare, hotel, and transportation to and from the airport—(read the section "Packages for the Independent Traveler," below). But if a package isn't for you and you need to book your airfare on your own, keep in mind these money-saving tips:

- *When* **you fly makes all the difference.** If you fly in late spring, summer, and early fall, you're guaranteed reductions on airfares to the Turks and Caicos. Passengers who can book their tickets long in advance, who stay over Saturday night, who fly midweek or at less-trafficked hours, or who travel during the off-season will likely pay a fraction of the full fare. If your schedule is flexible, say so, and ask if you can secure a cheaper fare by changing your flight plans.
- **Buy early.** The cheapest seats are often snagged by the early birds, so book as far in advance as possible.
- **Search the Internet for cheap fares.** Just plug in a destination and travel dates and times, and popular travel search sites such as Kayak.com will sift through thousands of airline websites and online travel agencies to track down the lowest airfares. In addition, many airline websites offer online-only discounted fares.
- **Keep an eye out for sales.** Check newspapers for advertised discounts or call the airlines directly and ask if any promotional rates or special fares are available. *Note:* The lowest-priced fares are often nonrefundable, require advance purchase of 1 to 3 weeks and a certain length of stay, and carry penalties for changing dates of travel.
- **Consolidators,** also known as bucket shops, are great sources for international tickets. Start by looking in Sunday newspaper travel sections; U.S. travelers should focus on the *New York Times, Los Angeles Times,* and *Miami Herald.* U.K. travelers should search in the *Independent,* the *Guardian,* or the *Observer.* For less-developed destinations, small travel agencies that cater to immigrant communities in large cities often have the best deals. *Beware:* Bucket-shop tickets are usually nonrefundable or rigged with stiff cancellation penalties, often as high as 50% to 75% of the ticket price, and some put you on charter airlines, which may leave at inconvenient times and experience delays. Several reliable consolidators are worldwide and available online. **STA Travel** has been the world's leading consolidator for students since purchasing Council Travel, but their fares are competitive for travelers of all ages. **Flights.com** (© **800/TRAV-800;** www.flights.com) has excellent fares worldwide, particularly to Europe. Its also has "local" websites in 12 countries. **Lowestfare.com** (© **800/FLY-CHEAP;** www. 1800flycheap.com), owned by package-holiday megalith MyTravel, has especially good fares to sunny destinations. **AirTicketsDirect** (© **800/858-8884;** www.airticketsdirect.com) is based in Montreal.
- **Join frequent-flier clubs.** Frequent-flier membership doesn't cost a cent, but it does entitle you to better seats, faster response to phone inquiries, and prompter service if your luggage is stolen or

your flight is canceled or delayed, or if you want to change your seat. And you don't have to fly to earn points; **frequent-flier credit cards** can earn you thousands of miles for doing your everyday shopping. With more than 70 mileage-awards programs on the market, consumers have never had more options. Investigate the program details of your favorite airlines before you sink points into any one. Consider which airlines have hubs in the airport nearest you, and, of those carriers, which have the most advantageous alliances, given your most common routes. To play the frequent-flier game to your best advantage, consult Randy Petersen's **Inside Flyer** (www.inside flyer.com). Petersen and friends review all the programs in detail and post regular updates on changes in policies and trends.

GETTING AROUND THE TURKS & CAICOS ISLANDS

Your most likely point of entry into the Turks and Caicos Islands will be the Providenciales International Airport. Depending on your final destination, from there you will take a taxi or rental car or hop on another flight. Please keep in mind, however, that interisland travel and brisk efficiency are not necessarily synonymous; the weather has a lot to do with it, but so does the sleepy-lidded pace of things. Get a couple of good books and just cozy up to that velvety breeze.

Note: In general, addresses have no street numbers, more typically just designations like "Leeward Highway," "Lower Bight Road," or simply "Providenciales."

For more information on getting around in Grand Turk and Salt Cay, go to chapter 6.

Getting Around Providenciales
From the Airport
Most of Provo's lodgings are an easy 15- to 20-minute taxi ride from the airport. The days of the free hotel **transfers** to and from the airport are pretty much over—your hotel can arrange a taxi transfer but for a charge (or the fee will be rolled into your rate); otherwise, plenty of **taxis** are on hand to meet arriving flights. If for some reason none are around, call your hotel or the **Provo Taxi Association** (© 649/946-5481). Cabs are metered and rates set by the government—but not all taxi drivers turn on their meters, so it's a good idea to negotiate the fare before you leave the airport—or anytime, for that matter. Expect to pay around $22 to $25 (plus tip) per couple (additional person $7.50) for a taxi ride from the airport to the Grace Bay area. Most taxis are vans equipped to carry more than one group of passengers, so it stands to reason that the more people on board, the lower the rate per couple.

Because the island is so large and its hotels and restaurants are so far-flung, you might find a **rental car** useful on Providenciales, but be warned: Renting a car on the TCI is not cheap. The airport has several rental-car agencies (see "Rental Cars," below).

Taxis

If you decide to forgo a rental car, you may find yourself needing a taxi every now and then, to get back to your hotel after dinner out, for example. Taxis are expensive—just jumping from one section of Grace Bay to another can run into double figures—and they're plentiful on Provo, but there are no designated taxi stands. We've hailed taxis down in the road a number of occasions, however. Or just have your hotel or restaurant call one for you. We also highly recommend Clayton Cox of **3 C's Taxi Service** (© 649/244-1546), **Lorenzo's Taxi & Tours** (© 649/243-8907), **Gray's Taxi & Tours** (© 649/242-3166), and **Boy Hall & Son Taxi** (© 649/244-3894 or 649/231-6308). If you find a taxi driver you like, ask for his or her card or jot down the number on the side of the van, and avail yourself of his or her services throughout your trip (taxi drivers are also happy to show you around the island—be sure to negotiate the fee upfront). Some Provo hotels (the Grace Bay Club being one) include complimentary shuttle service around the Grace Bay area. Otherwise, most places are happy to call a taxi for you.

Rental Cars

Three major U.S.–based car-rental agencies with a franchise in the Turks and Caicos Islands are **Budget,** with two Provo locations: the airport and Downtown Provo, in the Town Centre Mall (© 800/472-3325 in the U.S., or 649/946-4079, -5400; www.budgetrentacar.com); **Avis,** with a branch at the airport (© 800/331-1212 in the U.S. and Canada, or 649/946-4705; www.avis.tc); and **Hertz** affiliate **Mystique Car Rental,** located at the Ports of Call shopping complex on Grace Bay Road and on Old Airport Road, 2 minutes from the airport (© 649/941-3910; www.hertztci.com). Cars rent for $40 to $225 a day (depending on the vehicle); collision-damage insurance costs $10 to $12 a day. The government will collect a $16 tax for each rental contract, regardless of the number of days you keep the car. For booking rental cars online, the best deals are usually found at rental-car company websites, although all the major online travel agencies also offer rental-car reservations services.

If you'd like to try your luck with a local agency, call one of the following: **Grace Bay Car Rentals and Sales** (© 649/941-8500; www.gracebaycarrentals.com), on Grace Bay Road across from the Seven Stars resort; **Scooter Bob's,** Turtle Cove Marina (© 649/946-4684; www.provo.net/scooter), which rents jeeps, vans, and SUVs;

Tips **Renting a Car in Provo: Pros & Cons**

Many visitors wonder whether renting a car is the thing to do when in Provo. Some things to consider:

Pros:

- You can easily tour the island, go to shops, and eat out and not have to walk long distances to get places, or worry about relying on taxis.
- You can pick up supplies and food (especially if you have self-catering capabilities) from the Graceway Gourmet, the Graceway IGA, and other food suppliers with ease.
- Taxis are pricey!

Cons:

- If you're North American, you have to quickly master the nuances of left-side driving and navigating roundabouts.
- Parking is limited at many resorts. Some hotels offset this issue by providing complimentary transportation around the Grace Bay area for guests without cars.
- Most, if not all, tour operators include hotel pickup as part of their excursion packages.
- Bike riding is an ideal way to get around and perfectly meshes with the eco-friendly island vibe. Some resorts offer complimentary bikes. Or you can rent a bike or a scooter through Caicos Wheels; see below).
- Taxis are plentiful. Plus, more cars mean more congestion.
- Rental cars can be pricey!

Turks & Caicos National Car Rental (© 649/946-4701; http://airportinntci.com/rent), which has a branch at the Airport Plaza on Airport Road (2 min. from the airport); and **Rent a Buggy** (© 649/946-4158; www.rentabuggy.tc) on Leeward Highway, near Central Square. Most of these agencies offer free pickup and drop-off. Rates average from $40 to $200 per day, plus a $15 government tax.

In the British tradition, **cars on all the islands drive on the left.** You only need a valid driver's license from your home country to rent a vehicle.

Bicycles & Scooters

Bicycling is an ideal way to get around the flat Grace Bay area, especially now that the roads have been beautifully paved with nice sidewalks running on both sides. Many resorts, including Royal West Indies, the Grace Bay Club, and the Sands at Grace Bay, offer complimentary bikes for their guests. Now a new operator, **Caicos Wheels** (Queens Landing Plaza, Grace Bay; ℭ **649/242-6592;** www.caicoswheels. com), rents bikes (as well as scooters) in Providenciales. It will drop off and pick up bicycles at your resort; bikes cost $15 per day (deposit required).

In addition to cars, jeeps, and SUVs, **Scooter Bob's** (Turtle Cove Marina; ℭ **649/946-4684;** www.provo.net/scooter) rents two-passenger Yamaha scooters for $49 a day ($45 a day for 5 days or more). Advance reservations are required.

On Grand Turk, you can rent scooters and bikes at **Tony's Rentals** (ℭ **649/946-1879;** www.tonyscarrental.com).

On Foot

The 19km (12 miles) of Grace Bay Beach make for lovely strolls, and the nicely paved roads along Grace Bay have sidewalks, so getting around on foot is much easier than before. But once you get started, particularly with the tropical sun beating down, keep in mind that the distances are longer than they appear on a map—why not take the beach route instead and soak in the views while you're strolling?

Traveling on to the Other Islands

If your final destination is any of the other TCI islands, you will be taking either a **domestic flight** on a small plane from the Provo airport or traveling **by boat** (generally from Walkin Marina at Heaving Down Rock, in Leeward on Provo's northeast coast, about 20 min. from the airport; to get there you'll need to take a taxi from the airport if your hotel doesn't offer airport transfers).

At press time, the newest interisland charter airline is **Caicos Express** (ℭ **649/244-1407;** caicosexpressairways@tciway.tc).

Keep in mind that most of these small airlines have **weight restrictions,** which means you may have to store any heavier luggage in the Provo airport during your trip.

Caicos Cays: Getting There & Getting Around

The Caicos Cays are reachable by **boat, private plane,** or **air taxi;** Pine Cay has a tiny airstrip that's used by island homeowners and Meridian Club guests. Guests staying 7 nights or more at Pine Cay's Meridian Club enjoy complimentary air-taxi transfers from the Provo airport and boat transfers to and from the island. The charter company **Global Airways** (ℭ **649/941-3222;** www.globalairways.tc) also flies to Pine Cay. The Parrot Cay resort arranges taxi and boat transfers for its guests from the Provo airport. A number of the uninhabited cays, such as Fort George Cay and Little Water Cay, are destinations on many local tour-boat operators' half-day and full-day beach excursions.

Causeway Linking North & Middle Caicos

A long-awaited causeway linking North and Middle Caicos opened in late 2007, replacing the weekend ferry service between Bottle Creek on North Caicos and Middle Caicos. The 40m (130-ft.) causeway was dedicated to two men, Marco Delroy Williams and Javern Stacey Misick, who died when their boat sank in the creek in January 2007. *Note:* The causeway was severely damaged during the hurricanes of 2008; it has since been reopened, although residents complain that repairs were rudimentary and while crossable, the causeway still needs work.

North Caicos: Getting There & Getting Around

You can fly to the North Caicos airstrip on **Air Turks & Caicos** (formerly Interisland Airways) (© **649/946-4999;** www.airturksandcaicos.com); the 10-minute flights from Provo run Monday and Thursday only and cost $90 round-trip. The charter company **Global Airways** (© **649/941-3222;** www.globalairways.tc) also flies to North; call for updated fares.

We prefer to take the ferry to North Caicos; it's more convenient and cheaper. **TCI Ferry Service,** run by Caribbean Cruisin' Ltd. (© **649/946-5406,** cellphone 649/231-4191; www.caicosproperties. tc/TCIFerryService.html; $40 round-trip, cash only), offers a ferry service that travels between Provo's Walkin Marina (Heaving Down Rock, Leeward) and North Caicos five times a day from Monday to Saturday and makes three trips on Sunday; the trip is 25 to 30 minutes long. Otherwise, you can get to North Caicos by chartering a water-taxi from one of the many tour-boat operators in the area; it's not cheap, however. Try **Big Blue Unlimited** (© **649/946-5034;** www.bigblue.tc; $300 one-way; boat can accommodate up to eight people); the trip takes around 35 minutes. For ground transportation, call **Gardiner's Taxi** (© **649/946-7141**).

Middle Caicos: Getting There & Getting Around

The minuscule Middle Caicos airstrip no longer receives flights from **Air Turks & Caicos.** The charter company **Global Airways** (© **649/ 231-0045;** www.globalairways.tc) will fly you there for $500 one-way; the flight takes approximately 15 minutes. A much less expensive way to get to Middle is to take the ferry from Provo to North Caicos (see above) and then rent a car (or hire a taxi) and drive through North Caicos to Middle—that way you get to experience North as well! A great way to see Middle Caicos is on a full-day

"Heart of the Islands" eco-tour ($275/per person) or bike trip ($255/ per person) with **Big Blue** (✆ **649/946-5034;** www.bigblue.tc). Middle Caicos native and guide extraordinaire **Cardinal Arthur** (✆ **649/946-6107;** cellphone 649/241-0730) offers ground transportation, island and cave tours, boat excursions, and fishing expeditions.

South Caicos: Getting There & Getting Around

Air Turks & Caicos (✆ **649/946-4999;** www.airturksandcaicos. com) flies daily to South Caicos from Provo; flights cost $116 and take 20 to 25 minutes. Taxis are available at the airport.

Grand Turk: Getting There & Getting Around

Most people fly into Providenciales and then take a short flight on a domestic airline into Grand Turk International Airport (also known as J.A.G.S. McCartney International Airport). Several daily flights between Provo and Grand Turk are offered by **Air Turks & Caicos** (✆ **649/946-4999** or 649/946-1667 on Grand Turk; www.airturks andcaicos.com). The flight from Provo to Grand Turk takes 25 minutes and costs $135 to $160 round-trip.

On Grand Turk you can rent cars (as well as scooters, bicycles, and snorkeling gear) at **Tony's Car Rental** (Grand Turk International Airport; ✆ **649/964-1979;** www.tonyscarrental.com). Cars and jeeps cost $70 to $95 a day, scooter rentals cost $40 a day, and bike rentals are $20 a day. Tony's also offers scooter tours of the island.

Taxis are always available at the Grand Turk airport, and drivers are more than happy to give visitors a tour of the island; expect to pay around $50 to $60 for a 45-minute island tour.

For more information on getting to and getting around Grand Turk, see chapter 6.

Salt Cay: Getting There & Getting Around

The notoriously tiny airstrip at the Salt Cay airport has been lengthened and resurfaced—but you still need to arrive during daylight hours; the airstrip is not lighted for night. **Air Turks & Caicos** (✆ **649/946-4999** or 649/946-6940 or -6906 on Salt Cay; www.air turksandcaicos.com) and fly to Salt Cay from Providenciales. Or you can charter a flight with **Global Airways** (✆ **649/231-0045;** www. globalairways.tc) or **Caicos Express** (✆ **649/244-1407;** caicosexpress airways@tciway.tc).

Air Turks & Caicos offers daily flights between Provo and Salt Cay; the flight takes 30 minutes and costs $160. Contact Global for schedules and fees.

A government-subsidized **ferry** runs between Grand Turk and Salt Cay, weather permitting, every Tuesday, Wednesday, and Friday (leaving from South Dock—the island's *only* dock, by the way). The trip takes an hour and costs $12. You can also hire a **private boat operator** to take you between Salt Cay and Grand Turk (as long as the seas aren't too rough). Hire a boat charter with **Salt Cay Adventure Tours** (✆ 649/946-6909; www.saltcaytours.com). **Cruise-ship passengers** who arrive in Grand Turk can also contact Salt Cay Adventures to arrange day trips to Salt Cay.

No one needs a car to get around Salt Cay, which has more donkeys than cars to begin with; it's the perfect place for getting around on foot, by bike, or by golf cart. Contact **Salt Cay Riders Golf Cart Rentals** (✆ 649/244-1407; two-seater golf carts $65/day, $350/week; credit cards accepted).

For more information on getting to and getting around Salt Cay, see chapter 6.

---

7 MONEY & COSTS

CASH/CURRENCY The U.S. dollar is the legal currency of the Turks and Caicos. Traveler's checks are accepted at most places, as are Visa, MasterCard, and American Express.

ATMS/ABMS The easiest and best way to get cash away from home is from an ATM. For information on locations and opening times of ATMs (also known as ABMs) on the islands, see chapter 7.

Be sure you know your personal identification number (PIN) and your daily withdrawal limit before you leave home. Also keep in mind that many banks impose a fee every time a card is used at a different bank's ATM, and that fee is often higher for international transactions than for domestic ones. And if you use a debit card, the fees may be higher still—again, check with your bank before you leave home. On top of this, the bank from which you withdraw cash may charge its

---

> ⓘ **Tips** **Small Bills & Loose Change**
>
> Provo has an increasing number of ATMs (aka ABMs), but don't expect to find a cash machine on every street corner— and the other islands may have only one or two ATMs total (or none, in the case of North and Middle Caicos). So if you plan to travel to some of the less developed islands, it's a good idea to bring plenty of petty cash (small bills and loose change) for snacks, incidentals, and gratuities. Note that the Provo airport finally has an ATM; the Scotiabank cash machine is located in the airport check-in hall.

own fee. For international withdrawal fees, contact your bank for the details before you leave home.

TRAVELER'S CHECKS   You can get traveler's checks at almost any bank. They are offered in denominations of $20, $50, $100, $500, and sometimes $1,000. Generally, you'll pay a service charge ranging from 1% to 4%.

The most popular traveler's checks are offered by American Express (© **800/807-6233** or 800/221-7282 for cardholders—this number accepts collect calls, offers service in several foreign languages, and exempts Amex gold and platinum cardholders from the 1% fee); **Visa** (© **800/732-1322**)—AAA members can obtain Visa checks for a $9.95 fee (for checks up to $1,500) at most AAA offices or by calling © **866/339-3378;** and **MasterCard** (© **800/223-9920**).

If you carry traveler's checks, be sure to keep a record of their serial numbers separate from your checks in the event that they are stolen or lost. You'll get a refund faster if you know the numbers.

CREDIT CARDS   Credit cards are a safe way to carry money, they provide a convenient record of all your expenses, and they generally offer relatively good exchange rates. You can also withdraw cash advances from your credit cards at banks or ATMs, provided you know your PIN. Keep in mind that you'll pay interest from the moment of your withdrawal, even if you pay your monthly bills on time. Also note that many banks now assess a 1% to 3% "transaction fee" on all charges you incur abroad (whether you're using the local currency or your native currency).

Almost every credit card company has an emergency toll-free number that you can call if your wallet or purse is stolen. Credit card companies may be able to wire cash advances immediately, and in many places they can deliver an emergency credit card in a day or two. **Citicorp Visa**'s U.S. emergency number is © **800/336-8472.** **American Express** cardholders and traveler's check holders should call © **800/221-7282** for all money emergencies. **MasterCard** holders should call © **800/307-7309.**

8 HEALTH

The Turks and Caicos Islands are great for the soul but may be even better for the body. The TCI has no poisonous snakes or spiders, no malaria or other tropical diseases, is rabies-free, and boasts one of the lowest crime rates in the Caribbean. The wildest animals you'll find here are the islands' "potcake" dogs (see "Take Home a Potcake . . . or Two," below), which are generally as gentle as lambs. The waters are protected by a coral reef that rings the islands, so big waves and rough, turbulent surf are rare; in fact, the sea is often so gentle and clear (and the sandy bottom so free of rocks) that this is the perfect spot to teach toddlers and young children how to swim.

The exciting news on the TCI health front was the opening of the nation's **first hospital**. In April 2010, the **Turks & Caicos Island Hospital,** the nation's first modern hospital, opened its two centers: the **Cheshire Hall Medical Centre** (on Providenciales) and the **Cockburn Town Medical Center** (on Grand Turk).

Keep the following suggestions in mind to stay healthy and safe on your trip:

- **Be mindful of the tropical sun.** Wear sunglasses and a hat and use sunscreen liberally. Limit your time on the beach the first day. If you do overexpose yourself, stay out of the sun until you recover. If your exposure is followed by fever or chills, a headache, or a feeling of nausea or dizziness, see a doctor. And keep hydrated: Drink lots of water if you plan to be outside for long periods.
- **Bring insect repellent.** Fortunately, malaria-carrying mosquitoes in the Caribbean are confined largely to Haiti and the Dominican Republic. In the early evening, the witching hour for no-see-'ums, it's a good idea to spray on insect repellent (most restaurants have outdoor seating and often have insect-repellent spray on hand).
- **Be mindful of diving risks.** The Turks and Caicos is a diver's paradise. One of the more serious risks associated with diving is decompression sickness—more commonly known as "the bends." Associated Medical Practices (located in the Medical Building on Leeward Hwy. in Providenciales; © 649/946-4242) has a dive decompression chamber to treat the bends. *Note:* The treatment is expensive, so be sure to check your dive insurance before you make the plunge.
- **Consider drinking bottled water during your trip.** If you experience diarrhea, moderate your eating habits and drink only bottled water until you recover. If symptoms persist, consult a doctor.
- **Pack prescription medications in your carry-on luggage.** Carry written prescriptions in generic—not brand-name—form, and dispense all prescription medications from their original labeled vials. Many people try to carry drugs via prescription containers; Customs officials are aware of this type of smuggling and often check medication bottles. (***Exception:*** Liquid prescriptions *must* be in their original containers, per the latest Transportation Security Administration regulations.)
- **Pack an extra pair of contact lenses** (if you wear them), in case you lose one set.

Contact the **International Association for Medical Assistance to Travelers (IAMAT;** © **716/754-4883,** or in Canada 416/652-0137;

www.iamat.org) for tips on travel and health concerns on the islands you're visiting and lists of local English-speaking doctors. The **United States' Centers for Disease Control and Prevention** (© 800/311-3435; www.cdc.gov) provides up-to-date information on health hazards by region or country and offers tips on food safety. The website **www.tripprep.com**, sponsored by a consortium of travel-medicine practitioners, may also offer helpful advice.

What to Do if You Get Sick Away from Home

Finding a good doctor in the Turks and Caicos is not a problem, and most speak English. See chapter 7 for contact information on **hospitals, emergency numbers,** and **doctors** and **dentists.**

If you suffer from a chronic illness, consult your doctor before your departure. If you worry about getting sick away from home, you might want to consider medical travel insurance (see the section on travel insurance in chapter 7).

9 CRIME & SAFETY

The TCI has long been one of the safest places to live and visit in the Caribbean, but the recession has brought with it something entirely new to these islands: unemployment. And with it has come a slight uptick in petty crime. Some have attributed the trend as a natural by-product of development; others believe the changing population dynamics—the influx of a non-national workforce—is at work, although the global financial downturn and constitutional crisis are certainly factors. The bottom line: Crime is minimal in the islands—the locals, used to a world of unlocked doors, are deeply offended when someone resorts to robbing people of their possessions—but petty theft does take place, so protect your valuables, money, and cameras. Don't flash big wads of money around, especially when you arrive at the airport. Use common sense and be aware of your surroundings at all times. Keep your doors locked.

10 SPECIALIZED TRAVEL RESOURCES

TRAVELERS WITH DISABILITIES

Many resorts, condos, and villas in the Turks and Caicos are wheelchair accessible. We've indicated this in the amenities section of the hotel reviews.

Take Home a Potcake . . . or Two

The homeless dogs you see roaming the streets of many Caribbean countries generally stay that way: homeless and constantly foraging for food and shelter. The **Turks & Caicos Society for the Prevention of Cruelty to Animals (TCSPCA)** was founded in 2000 to better address the plight of these homeless dogs, here called "potcakes"—the name comes from the food once fed to stray dogs, the caked remains at the bottom of cooking pots. And they've succeeded to a large degree on Provo: You rarely see collarless potcakes running lickety-split along the beach (the Environmental Health department has been cracking down, some say a little too zealously). Many people who've adopted potcakes find that they're smart, unflappable, incredibly adaptable and loving dogs. Potcakes look like the ultimate mutts, with floppy ears and tan or black markings; many a visitor has fallen in love during a stay in the TCI. Along with lobbying the government to adopt animal protection laws and create an animal control unit, the TCSPCA has been able to find homes for many of these dogs all over the world. The TCSPCA has been instrumental in promoting "off-island adoptions," making it easy for visitors to actually carry home a potcake puppy (the TCI has no pet quarantine periods coming in or going out of the country). Every puppy comes with shots and medical certificates and can be carried in the passenger cabins of most airplanes. For more information, contact the TCSPCA (© 649/941-8846; http://tcspca.tc) or the island charity set up to improve the lives of TCI potcakes, the **Potcake Foundation** (www.potcakefoundation.com). The **Potcake Place** is a nonprofit rescue organization (© 649/231-1010; www.potcakeplace.com).

Many travel agencies offer customized tours and itineraries for travelers with disabilities. **Flying Wheels Travel** (© 507/451-5005; www.flyingwheelstravel.com) offers escorted tours and cruises that emphasize sports and private tours in minivans with lifts. **Access-Able Travel Source** (© 303/232-2979; www.access-able.com) offers extensive access information and advice for traveling around the world with disabilities.

Avis Rent a Car has an "Avis Access" program that offers such services as a dedicated 24-hour toll-free number (© **888/879-4273**) for customers with special travel needs; special car features such as swivel seats, spinner knobs, and hand controls; and accessible bus service.

Organizations that offer assistance to travelers with disabilities include **MossRehab** (www.mossresourcenet.org), which provides a library of accessible-travel resources online; **SATH** (Society for Accessible Travel & Hospitality; © **212/447-7284;** www.sath.org), which offers a wealth of travel resources for all types of disabilities and informed recommendations on destinations, access guides, travel agents, tour operators, vehicle rentals, and companion services; and the **American Foundation for the Blind** (AFB; © **800/232-5463;** www.afb.org), a referral resource for the blind or visually impaired that includes information on traveling with Seeing Eye dogs.

Also check out the quarterly magazine *Emerging Horizons* (www.emerginghorizons.com) and *Open World* magazine, published by SATH (see above).

GAY & LESBIAN TRAVELERS

The **International Gay and Lesbian Travel Association** (IGLTA; © 954/776-2626; www.iglta.org) is the trade association for the gay and lesbian travel industry, and offers an online directory of gay- and lesbian-friendly travel businesses; go to its website and click on "Members."

SENIOR TRAVEL

Members of **AARP,** 601 E St. NW, Washington, DC 20049 (© **888/687-2277;** www.aarp.org), get discounts on hotels, airfares, and car rentals. AARP offers members a wide range of benefits, including *AARP The Magazine* and a monthly newsletter. Anyone over 50 can join.

Recommended publications offering travel resources and discounts for seniors include: the quarterly magazine *Travel 50 & Beyond* (www.travel50andbeyond.com) and the bestselling paperback *Unbelievably Good Deals and Great Adventures That You Absolutely Can't Get Unless You're Over 50 2007–2008, 17th Edition* (McGraw-Hill), by Joan Rattner Heilman.

FAMILY TRAVEL

The TCI is highly recommended as a family destination. Hotels and resorts by and large welcome families with open arms, and even those with specific adults-only aspects have developed delightful kid-friendly amenities and programs. The gentle, clear, shallow waters and soft-sand beaches of the TCI are particularly attractive for families with toddlers and young children, and older kids will have plenty of nonmotorized

Tips   Baby-Equipment Rentals

Most hotels and resorts in Provo are happy to provide cribs, highchairs, and other baby equipment. (Amanyara even provides parents with Diaper Champs, toddler potties, and homemade baby food!) If you're renting a villa or condo, however, you may need to rent baby equipment. **Happy Na** (the owner's name is Naomi) has baby-equipment rentals (cribs, car seats, highchairs, and playpens), as well as baby gifts. They're located at Southwinds Plaza on Leeward Highway in Provo (*©* **649/941-3568** daytime or 649/941-5326 evenings). Cribs rent for $8 to $20 a day. The shop will deliver equipment 7 days a week from 9am to 8pm.

watersports activities (snorkeling, sailing, parasailing) to keep them happy. One thing you don't find in the TCI, however, is video-game arcades or similar venues where young teens congregate.

11 RESPONSIBLE TOURISM

For the TCI, sustainability of resources is not just a fashionable notion; it's basic survival. For centuries, island inhabitants have had to make do with the resources available to them. The land is largely arid and sandy; rainfall is sparse and fresh water a scarce and precious commodity.

So far, the government's emphasis on **high-end, low-impact tourism** has worked to temper the impact of rapid development and helped to maintain the delicate balance between commercial interests and environmental ones. Height limits set up for resorts along Grace Bay (famously breached before the recession hit by one brash, high-flying property) helped stem the dreaded coastal phenomenon known as the "New Jersey-ization" of the shoreline. Most of the newer resorts have even implemented their own eco-initiatives. The West Bay Club has its own waste-treatment system and recycles gray water (wastewater from dish, shower, and sink, and laundry water) for landscaping purposes. Each room in the Gansevoort is equipped with an Energy Management System (electricity is turned on with your room key), and a high-efficiency central air-conditioning system reduces consumption by 30%.

Of utmost importance to the nation is the maintenance of its most precious natural resource: the pristine **marine environment,** which

General Resources for Responsible Travel

The following websites provide valuable wide-ranging information on sustainable travel.

- **Responsible Travel** (www.responsibletravel.com) is a great source of sustainable travel ideas; the site is run by a spokesperson for ethical tourism in the travel industry. **Sustainable Travel International** (www.sustainabletravelinternational.org) promotes ethical tourism practices, and manages an extensive directory of sustainable properties and tour operators around the world.

- **Carbonfund** (www.carbonfund.org), **TerraPass** (www.terrapass.org), and **Cool Climate** (http://coolclimate.berkeley.edu) provide info on "carbon offsetting," or offsetting the greenhouse gas emitted during flights.

- **Greenhotels** (www.greenhotels.com) recommends green-rated member hotels around the world that fulfill the company's stringent environmental requirements. **Environmentally Friendly Hotels** (www.environmentallyfriendlyhotels.com) offers more green accommodation ratings.

- **Volunteer International** (www.volunteerinternational.org) has a list of questions to help you determine the intentions and the nature of a volunteer program. For general info on volunteer travel, visit **www.volunteerabroad.org** and **www.idealist.org**.

includes the spectacular **coral reef system.** Maintaining the current status quo is paramount to preventing a "slide towards another spoiled paradise," says Mark Parrish, owner of the watersports operator and eco-pioneer Big Blue Unlimited. "The islands are still beautiful, the seas are still clean, and the reefs are the cornerstone of life," Parrish says. "The future of the TCI must lie in the proper management of the environment and in eco-tourism." Visitors can help out, Parrish suggests, by choosing low-impact excursions.

Eco-tourism got a big boost here when the entire Grace Bay area was awarded **national marine park status.** No commercial or sport fishing is allowed in the protected 2,630-hectare (6,500-acre) Princess Alexandra National Park. No jet-ski central this; and hopefully never will be. National marine parks have been established on and around just about every island on the TCI; for a full list of protected areas, go to the **Department of Environment and Coastal Services** website at **www.environment.tc**. Even outside park boundaries, mooring buoys have been established at all dive sites and mooring areas to avoid possible damage from anchors. TCI dive operators are a particularly enlightened bunch in regards to reef preservation and resource conservation.

The scarcity of **fresh water** has always been an issue on these islands—never more so than now with the growing influx of visitors. To prevent water shortages, **modern reverse osmosis plants** have been constructed on Provo and Grand Turk.

The daily air importation of **fresh food** to meet the needs of the tourist population is leaving a hefty carbon footprint, however. It's been estimated that a whopping 90% of food consumed on the island is imported from the U.S., Haiti, and the Dominican Republic—with a whopping annual price tag to match: The *Turks & Caicos Free Press* reported that in 2008–9 the food import bill came to around $63 million. That's why it's so heartening to hear that agriculture is undergoing a revival in the Turks and Caicos. In the fertile soil of North Caicos—traditionally the breadbasket of the TCI, raising fruits and vegetables for TCI inhabitants throughout the 20th century—farmers are getting a boost from government initiatives. Subsidies are reviving a 143-acre **working farm** in Kew, which is growing and selling produce in North Caicos and a small farmer's market in Provo. (We saw peppadews, beans, and fresh pigeon peas on a recent visit.) Demonstration plots have shown the productive potential of North Caicos soil: Growing in abundance are tomatoes, cucumbers, peppers, cabbages, fruits (papayas, mangoes, bananas, melons), even herbs. And retailers are responding: In 2010, Gemma Handy in the *Turks and Caicos Weekly News* reported that the IGA Graceway supermarket in Provo was buying up spectacular okra grown by septuagenarian farmer Emanuel Misick on his 20-acre Green Acre Farm in Bottle Creek.

12 PACKAGES FOR THE INDEPENDENT TRAVELER

For value-conscious travelers, packages are often a smart way to go because they can save you a ton of money. Package tours are *not* the same thing as escorted tours. You'll be on your own, but in most cases, an air/land/hotel package to TCI will include airfare, hotel, and car rental—and it'll cost you less than just the hotel alone if you booked it yourself.

You'll find packages to Turks and Caicos, but they aren't as common as for other Caribbean Islands (TCI has instead opted for upscale marketing). Check out some of the big **online travel agencies**—Expedia, Travelocity, and Orbitz—which do a brisk business in packages. Remember to comparison shop among at least three different operators, and always compare apples to apples.

One good source of package deals is the airlines themselves. Most major airlines offer air/land/hotel packages, including **American Airlines Vacations** (© 800/321-2121; www.aavacations.com), **Delta Vacations** (© 800/221-6666; www.deltavacations.com), **Continental Airlines Vacations** (© 800/301-3800; www.covacations.com), and **United Vacations** (© 888/854-3899; www.unitedvacations. com). **Liberty Travel** (© 888/271-1584; www.libertytravel.com) also occasionally offers packages to Turks and Caicos.

Of course, don't forget to check **hotel or resort websites** for very desirable package deals, especially in the off-season. No, these packages rarely include airfares, but they're packed with extra amenities (or a night free) if you book a block of vacation time, say, 5 or 7 days. These packages are often built around themes and often include meals, spa treatments, or excursions along with the lodging.

13 STAYING CONNECTED

WITHOUT YOUR OWN COMPUTER

Many **hotels** and **resorts** in the TCI feature "libraries" or small business centers where guests have complimentary use of computers with high-speed Internet access. The number of computers available is often limited, however, and you may have to wait your turn to use one.

WITH YOUR OWN COMPUTER

The wireless world (Wi-Fi) is up and rolling on the Turks and Caicos Islands; most resorts have wireless Internet access. For dial-up access, most business-class hotels offer dataports for laptop modems. In addition, major Internet service providers (ISPs) have **local access numbers** around the world, allowing you to go online by placing a local call. The **iPass** network also has dial-up numbers around the world. You'll have to sign up with an iPass provider, who will then tell you how to set up your computer for your destination(s). For a list of iPass providers, go to www.ipass.com and click on "Individuals Buy Now."

PLANNING YOUR TRIP TO TURKS & CAICOS

2

GETTING MARRIED IN TURKS & CAICOS

ⓘ Tips Calling Home

Making international calls from the Turks and Caicos can be costly, in particular if you're dialing direct from your hotel room, where you are charged more than $2 a minute. You cannot access most U.S. toll-free numbers from the TCI; for example, you won't be able to use AT&T prepaid calling cards here. You can use any GSM cellphone if it has international roaming capabilities. One way to avoid the high costs of calling home from your hotel room is to **buy a prepaid cellphone** in the TCI. You can purchase a cellphone for as low as $60; it comes with a $10 phone card. Additional prepaid phone cards come in $10, $20, $50, and $75 denominations. Phones and cards can be found at the **Cable & Wireless** offices on Leeward Highway (ⓒ **649/946-2200**) and at the Graceway IGA Supermarket (Cable & Wireless has a small office at the entrance). Another option is to **rent a cellphone. TCIonline Internet Café** (in the Ports of Call shopping center, Provo; ⓒ **649/941-4711**) offers cellphone rentals ($75 deposit; $7/day; $30/week; phone time is charged to your credit card as you use minutes), as do Grant's Texaco Downtown and Kathleen's 7-Eleven on Leeward Highway.

One solid provider is **i2roam** (www.i2roam.com; ⓒ **866/811-6209** or 920/235-0475).

---

14 GETTING MARRIED IN TURKS & CAICOS

As TCI's former premier, the Honorable Dr. Michael Misick, proved when he married Hollywood starlet LisaRaye McCoy (star of the UPN comedy *All of Us*) in 2006 in a celebrity-studded wedding at Amanyara, the Turks and Caicos Islands are a hot destination-wedding spot. (It's no guarantee that the marriage will last, alas; theirs didn't.) You can get married barefoot on the beach, in a ballroom at a luxury resort, on a sailboat, or in one of the island's colorful churches, to name a few choice scenarios. An increasing number of resorts and tour operators are equipped to handle weddings soup-to-nuts. Here is a sampling of options:

- **Sail Provo** (www.sailprovo.com) can organize a wedding on one of its large catamarans or on a secluded beach, with all the trimmings, for up to 100 people.
- The **Regent Palms** resort offers customized wedding services and your choice of ceremony locations (on the beach, in the Palms Court—which was featured in the Aug 2005 issue of *Modern Bride*—or in the Messel Ballroom) and reception locations (the Messel Ballroom, on the beachside wooden deck, or in the courtyard).
- **Beaches Turks & Caicos** (© 800/SANDALS [7263257]) marries couples on a regular basis—in high season as many as *80 couples a month*. It's big business for Beaches, and they take it very seriously, with an on-site wedding coordinator and complete wedding packages to choose from.

You need to meet the following legal requirements to marry in the TCI: You will need to bring a passport, a copy of your birth certificate, proof of status from your place of residence (if single, a sworn affidavit), and a divorce decree if you're divorced. You will need to pay a $100 license fee. You must be on island for 72 hours to establish residency, and the marriage license takes 2 to 3 days to process. *Note:* If you plan to marry in one of the island churches, you may need proof of membership.

The Turks and Caicos Islands marriage certificate is legally recognized in the U.S., Canada, and the U.K. For more details, contact the **Registry of Births, Deaths and Marriages** on Front Street at © **649/ 946-2800** in Grand Turk (the Registry also has an office in Provo at © **649/946-5350**).

---

15 TIPS ON ACCOMMODATIONS

SAVING ON YOUR HOTEL ROOM

The rates given in this book are only "rack rates"—that is, the officially posted rate that you'd be given if you just walked in off the street. Almost no one actually pays them. Always ask about packages and discounts. Comparison shop online for great deals on hotel rooms on hotel websites (which often offer multiday packages). Or check **Hotels.com, Travelocity, Expedia, Orbitz, Priceline,** and **Hotwire.**

It's a good idea to **get a confirmation number** and **make a printout** of any online-booking transaction.

The high season in the Turks and Caicos is the winter season, roughly from the middle of December through the middle of April. Hotels charge their highest rates during the winter season, and you'll need to make reservations months in advance to snag a room at your favorite hotel or resort during this peak period. The Christmas holidays have become big business for TCI lodgings, and you may need to reserve a year in advance for a room during this time.

The off-season in the TCI is the rest of the year—although the so-called "shoulder seasons," roughly late spring and late fall (after hurricane season is over)—are increasingly popular. Still, outside the traditional high season, expect rates to fall, sometimes dramatically in the summer.

WATCH OUT FOR THOSE EXTRAS! The government imposes a flat 11% occupancy tax, applicable to all hotels, guesthouses, and restaurants in the 40-island chain. When booking a room, ask whether the price you've been quoted includes the tax. That will avoid an unpleasant surprise when it comes time to pay the bill.

Furthermore, many hotels routinely add 10% to 12% for "service." That means that with tax and service, some bills are 17% or even 25% higher than the price that was originally quoted to you!

That's not all. Some hotels slip in little hidden extras that add up quickly. For example, it's common for many places to quote rates that include a continental breakfast. Should you prefer ham and eggs, you will pay extra charges. If you request special privileges, like extra towels for the beach or laundry done in a hurry, surcharges may mount. It pays to watch those extras and to ask questions before you commit.

One of the biggest extras is phone charges. Try to avoid making international calls from your hotel phone—you'll be charged around $2.10 a minute, depending on the time of day, which can add up quickly. Many hotels also have fees for local calls, sometimes $1 and up. If you have a GSM cellphone with international roaming capabilities, you're in business; otherwise, you may want to consider renting a cellphone or buying a prepaid cellphone when you're on island. See "Calling Home," above.

And don't forget gratuities. You will be expected to tip just about everyone who does a service for you, from the beach boy who sets up your beach chairs and towels to your masseuse to your captain (and any mates who are particularly helpful) on a beach cruise. Many hotels now have personal concierge service, and you should tip them at the end of your stay.

WHAT THE ABBREVIATIONS MEAN Rate sheets often have these classifications:

- **MAP (Modified American Plan)** usually means room, breakfast, and dinner, unless the room rate has been quoted separately, in which case it means only breakfast and dinner.

What Are Condo Hotels?

In the Turks and Caicos, the buzzword in resort development is **condo hotels.** Many, if not most, of the resorts on Grace Bay are fully or partially condo hotels. Condo hotels are nothing but hotels whose units are sold to individual owners, usually even before the hotel is built. Most units then enter the resort rental pool: When the owner is not using the unit, it is managed and rented out to hotel guests by the resort; the owner then receives a percentage of the rental income. This is a popular concept in the TCI for a number of reasons, one of which is the favorable financial conditions here for international investors, large and small, including no property taxes, capital gains taxes, or sales taxes.

- **CP (Continental Plan)** includes room and a light breakfast.
- **EP (European Plan)** means room only.
- **AP (American Plan)** includes your room plus three meals a day.

HOTELS & RESORTS   Many budget travelers assume they can't afford the big hotels and resorts. But there are so many packages out there (see the section "Packages for the Independent Traveler," earlier in this chapter) and so many advertised sales during the low season that you might be pleasantly surprised at what you can get. And many hotels offer upgrades whenever they have a big block of rooms to fill and few reservations.

ALL-INCLUSIVE RESORTS   The ideal all-inclusive is just that—a place where *everything*—meals, drinks, and most watersports—is included. In the Turks and Caicos, three resorts now bill themselves as all-inclusive: **Beaches**, **Club Med Turkoise,** and the **Veranda.** The all-inclusive market is geared to the active traveler who likes organized entertainment, lots of sports and workouts at fitness centers, and lots of food and drink—and all three resorts come through in these categories.

In the 1990s, so many competitors entered the all-inclusive market that the term means different things to the different resorts that embrace this marketing strategy. With the TCI all-inclusives, all meals, drinks, and gratuities are included, for example, but you'll have to pay for extras such as certain spa treatments or optional scuba-diving services. At the island's newest all-inclusive, the Veranda, menu items have prices attached—a neat bit of transparency that lets you know exactly what you're paying for.

The all-inclusives have a reputation for being expensive, but to many people not having to "pay as you go" or deal with gratuities is liberating and worth the money. If you're looking for ways to cut costs with an all-inclusive, the trick is to travel in off-peak periods, which doesn't always mean just from mid-April to mid-December. If you want a winter vacation at an all-inclusive, choose the month of January—not February or the Christmas holidays, when prices are at their all-year high. The resorts also regularly offer special packages for weeklong stays; check the websites for the latest offerings.

GUESTHOUSES/INNS An entirely different type of accommodations is the guesthouse. In the Caribbean the term "guesthouse" can mean anything. Sometimes so-called guesthouses are really like simple motels built around swimming pools. Others are small individual cottages, with their own kitchenettes, constructed around a main building in which you'll often find a bar and a restaurant that serves local food. Still others are more like small inns, often with private bathrooms, luxury linens, and boutique amenities. The guesthouse or inn usually represents very good value, simply because it does not have the full-service amenities of a resort or hotel.

In the TCI, you can find inns or guesthouses in Grand Turk, Salt Cay, North Caicos, Middle Caicos, and South Caicos .

RENTING A VILLA, CONDO, OR HOUSE Particularly if you're a family or a group of friends, a "housekeeping holiday" can be one of the least expensive ways to vacation in the Turks and Caicos, and if you like privacy and independence, it's a good way to go. Accommodations with kitchens are now available on nearly all the islands. Some are individual cottages, others are condo complexes with swimming pools, and many others are private homes that owners rent out. Many (though not all) places include maid service, and you're given fresh linens as well.

In the simpler rentals, doing your own cooking and laundry or even your own maid service may not be your idea of a good time in the sun, but it saves money—a lot of money. The savings, especially for a family of three to six people, or two or three couples, can range from 50% to 60% of what a hotel would cost. Groceries are sometimes priced 35% to 60% higher than on the U.S. mainland, as nearly all foodstuffs have to be imported, but even so, preparing your own food will be a lot cheaper than dining at restaurants.

There are also a number of quite lavish homes for rent for which you can spend a lot and stay in the lap of luxury in a prime beachfront setting. Many villas have a staff, or at least a maid who comes in a few days a week, and they also provide the essentials for home life, including linens and housewares. Condos usually come with a reception desk and are often comparable to a suite in a big resort hotel. Nearly all condo complexes have pools (some more than one). Like condos, villas range widely in price.

You'll have to approach these rental properties with a certain sense of independence. There may or may not be a front desk to answer your questions, and you'll have to plan your own watersports.

For a list of agencies that arrange rentals in Providenciales, see a few recommended options below. If you're looking for rentals in North or Middle Caicos, you can ask the Turks & Caicos Tourist Board for good suggestions. For villa rentals in Grand Turk and Salt Cay, see chapter 6.

Make your reservations well in advance. Here are a few agencies that rent in Provo:

- **North Shore Villas** (© **404/467-4858;** www.northshorevillas. com) has a number of deluxe free-standing private villas, most of which are located on Grace Bay Beach, as well as other vacation villa properties all over Provo.
- **Prestigious Properties** (© **649/946-4379;** http://prestigious properties.com) offers a range of villas, condos, and single-family residences.
- **Seafeathers Villas** (© **649/941-5703;** www.seafeathers.com) has a variety of beachfront villas, cottages, and condos, many with private pools and oceanfront locations. Chefs, maids, and babysitters are also available on request.
- **Ocean Point Villas** (© **404/467-4858;** www.oceanpointvillas. com) has lovely deluxe villas ranging in size from two to seven bedrooms in the strictly residential neighborhood of Ocean Point and on the North Shore near Turtle Cove.

3

Where to Stay in Providenciales & the Caicos Islands

The prevalence of high-end boutique resorts in Provo means that consumers looking for a budget island getaway should reserve well in advance for the handful of moderately priced options. It's also useful to be on the lookout for package deals on hotel websites, online travel-booking sites such as Orbitz, Expedia, and Travelocity, or massive travel search engines like Kayak and Mobissimo. Check this guide's hotel reviews before you book, and see what other travelers have to say about TCI lodgings on Frommers.com message boards.

In contrast to what's available on Provo and Parrot Cay and Pine Cay (two privately owned Caicos Cays islands with hotel resorts), moderately priced lodgings are currently the main option in the rest of the Caicos islands.

Keep in mind that the government imposes a mandatory 11% occupancy tax, and many resorts charge an additional service charge of 10% or more. Also note that during high season—and the Christmas/New Year's holidays in particular—resorts have minimum-stay requirements. Hotels throughout the Turks and Caicos accept most major credit cards, except where noted.

Finally, as you can see when comparing winter and summer rack rates listed below, visiting Provo in the off-season can be considerably more economical than a high-season winter vacation. The most expensive time to come is during the Christmas/New Year's holidays; check each resort's website for holiday rates. Be sure to look for money-saving online package deals any time of year.

For information on villa or apartment stays in Provo and the Caicos islands, see "Tips on Accommodations" in chapter 2.

1 PROVIDENCIALES

Provo's 19km (12-mile) Grace Bay is where most of the islands' resorts and hotels are situated. Provo's lodgings are an easy 10- to 15-minute taxi ride from the airport.

Comings & Goings

It's been a particularly dynamic time for resort business on the islands in light of the worldwide financial tumult and the homegrown constitutional crisis. At press time, the ultraluxe development project at **Dellis Cay**—a Caicos islet where six "starchitects" had been hired to design cutting-edge villas and movie stars like Michael Douglas were measuring for drapes—was in receivership. The "mac daddy" of luxury resorts, as one hotelier called it, simply went bust in hard times. Similarly, the construction of **Molasses Reef,** the luxury Ritz-Carlton resort complex on West Caicos, was on hold, perhaps permanently. The owner of **Nikki Beach,** a glitzy global resort brand whose luxury rooms cost as much as $3,000 a night, went into receivership in 2009 after less than 2 years in business on Leeward Beach; the property is currently up for sale. On the other hand, a number of handsome new properties opened for business on Provo in 2009–10, including the **Gansevoort,** the **Veranda,** and the **West Bay Club** (see all below). And construction on properties in the **Turks & Caicos Sporting Club** in Ambergris Cay (South Caicos) continues apace.

GRACE BAY
Very Expensive

Beaches Turks & Caicos Resort & Spa ★ (Kids)   This Grace Bay megaresort remains a perennial favorite among families. And with a whopping 453 units, it's remarkable that it all chugs along as smoothly as it does. The grounds are beautifully maintained, kids look deliriously happy, and weddings are held on-site on an almost daily basis. It's a winning formula: Rooms are nearly impossible to come by in high season without reservations made long in advance.

This resort is part of the Sandals chain of all-inclusive hotels, though unlike at most Sandals, families with kids are welcome here—and welcome with a bang. The all-inclusive designation means you get a lot for your money: all meals and drinks; excellent watersports; winning service from a huge staff of nearly 800 employees; a full-service nursery with cribs, swings, rockers, and a coterie of nannies with whom you can leave babies and toddlers; and even a spa, the **Red Lane** (daily 8am–8pm). "The Caribbean Adventure with Sesame Street" activities are available for kids 5 and under; actors dressed as characters from *Sesame Street*—Elmo and his friends—are on hand to thrill the little ones. The Kids Camp has daylong activities for children

6 to 12. The older kids can lose themselves in free, unlimited play at the Xbox 360 Game Garage interactive gaming center. Tweens and teens can groove to DJ-spun sounds (and vie for one of the four VIP cabanas) at Club Liquid.

Gratuities are included for everything, so you don't have to worry about carrying around small bills and change and doling out tips all day. If you've got a gambling itch, 24-hour slot machines are available on the patio near the Turtles Bar. Note, however, that you'll pay extra for many spa treatments, certain scuba-diving courses and island excursions, and international telephone calls.

Accommodations come in 12 different categories and a variety of configurations and bedrooms. The older part of the resort has been refreshed (the decor is spiffier in the French Village, the newer section).

(Tips) Finding Sundries on Grace Bay

For visitors who find they've forgotten an essential toiletry, crave a snack or a soft drink (and want to avoid paying through the nose in a resort restaurant or bar), or need sunscreen or bug repellent, the Grace Bay area can be a tough place to locate such little conveniences—unlike in North America, where 7-Elevens and other convenience stores and grocery chains are just around the corner. Vending machines are virtually nonexistent on Grace Bay. Cause for celebration is the recent opening of a full-service grocery store on Grace Bay. The **Graceway Gourmet (© 649/333-5000),** across the street from the Seven Stars Resort in central Grace Bay (at Dolphin Ave.), is impressively stocked and more conveniently located than its (larger) sister grocery store, the Graceway IGA, on Leeward Highway (reachable by car or taxi). The Graceway Gourmet has basic supplies, fresh produce, meats and seafood, a salad bar, a deli, a coffee bar, even Wi-Fi; it's open 7 days a week from 7am to 9pm. A few other well-placed convenience stores are within walking distance of most resorts in and around Grace Bay supply the essentials and more— including snacks and candy bars (all the familiar brands), beer, wine, and liquor, magazines, even local handicrafts. The following are open daily from around 9am to 6pm:

- **The Sand Dollar** at the Sands on Grace Bay
- **Sand Castle Convenience Store** at Ocean Club East
- **Neptune's Nectar** (in back of Ports of Call shopping village)

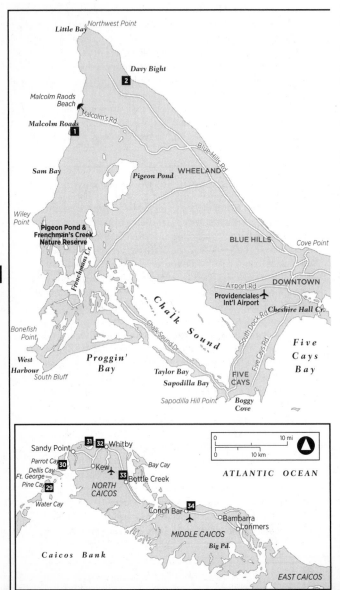

Little Bay
Northwest Point
Davy Bight
2
Malcolm Raods Beach
Malcolm's Rd.
Malcolm Roads
1
Blue Hills Rd.
Sam Bay
Pigeon Pond
WHEELAND
Wiley Point
Pigeon Pond & Frenchman's Creek Nature Reserve
BLUE HILLS
Cove Point
Frenchmans Cr.
Airport Rd
DOWNTOWN
Providenciales Int'l Airport
Bonefish Point
Chalk Sound
South Dock Rd
Cheshire Hall Cr.
Chalk Sound Dr.
Five Cays Bay
West Harbour
South Bluff
Proggin' Bay
Taylor Bay
Sapodilla Bay
FIVE CAYS
Five Cays Rd
Sapodilla Hill Point
Boggy Cove

31 **32** Whitby
Sandy Point
Parrot Cay **30**
Dellis Cay
Ft. George
Pine Cay **29**
Kew
33 Bottle Creek
NORTH CAICOS
Bay Cay
Water Cay
ATLANTIC OCEAN
0   10 mi
0   10 km
Conch Bar
34
Bambarra
Lorimers
MIDDLE CAICOS
Big Pd.
Caicos Bank
EAST CAICOS

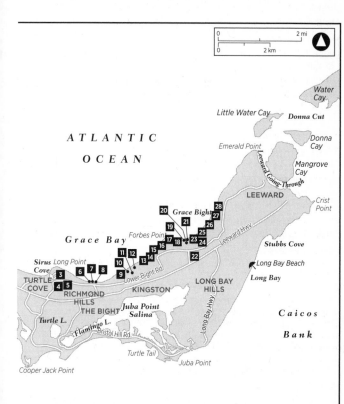

ATLANTIC OCEAN

Grace Bay

Forbes Point

Sirus Cove *Long Point*

TURTLE COVE

RICHMOND HILLS

THE BIGHT

Turtle L.

Flamingo L.

Bristol Hill Rd.

Turtle Tail

Cooper Jack Point

KINGSTON

Juba Point Salina

Juba Point

LONG BAY HILLS

Lower-Bight Rd.

Grace Bight

Leeward Hwy

LEEWARD

Emerald Point

Little Water Cay

Donna Cut

Water Cay

Donna Cay

Mangrove Cay

Leeward Going-Through

Crist Point

Stubbs Cove

Long Bay Beach

Long Bay

Long Bay Hwy.

Caicos Bank

0   2 mi
0   2 km

All rooms and suites have king-size beds. The higher-category suites have four-poster beds, a "Premium Bar" and fully stocked refrigerator based on your personal requests, and 8am to 8pm concierge service. The luxury suites offer a really nifty amenity: 24-hour butler service, with professionally trained butlers catering to your every need. The largest unit, the French Village three-bedroom suite, can accommodate up to 11 people. The resort's newest section, the all-suites **Italian Village,** featuring a 1,115-sq.-m (12,002-sq.-ft.) pool with a **giant water park** (with wave pool) and 168 spanking-new family suites, is open for business.

Food is available somewhere on the resort 24 hours a day, but room service is offered only in the butler-suite categories (see above). In general, the food is plentiful, if not particularly inspired. Among the 16 restaurants, you can get Italian **(Giuseppe),** Tex-Mex **(Arizona's),** seafood **(Schooners),** or Asian **(Kimonos). Reflections** offers casual-fare buffets for breakfast, lunch, and dinner. For the kids, the very cool **Bobby D's** is a 1950s-style diner with typical kid faves like burgers, hot dogs, and spaghetti. The resort's showcase restaurant, **Sapodilla's,** is adults-only and features Continental cuisine; reservations are recommended.

Lower Bight Rd. (P.O. Box 186), Providenciales, Turks and Caicos, B.W.I. © **800/ 232-2437** in the U.S. or 649/946-8000. Fax 649/946-8001. www.beaches.com. 620 units. Prices based on 2 nights (minimum stay): Winter $420–$510 double, $640 1-bedroom suite, $1,200 2-bedroom suite for 4, $1,680 3-bedroom family suite; off-season $385–$440 double, $575–$675 1-bedroom suite, $1,090 2-bedroom suite for 4, $1,525 3-bedroom family suite. Rates are all-inclusive. AE, DISC, MC, V. **Amenities:** 10 restaurants; 7 bars; babysitting; children's center w/pool; fitness center; basketball; volleyball; nurses' station; Internet café; 8 outdoor pools; 2 saunas; spa; 4 lighted tennis courts; watersports equipment (extensive). *In room:* A/C, ceiling fan, TV, CD players, fridge, hair dryer, in-room bars (in concierge rooms), Wi-Fi (free).

Club Med Turkoise ★ Set on 28 hectares (69 acres) of sun-blasted scrubland on a white strip of beachfront overlooking Grace Bay, this adults-only all-inclusive resort was one of the pioneers of Grace Bay when it opened in 1984. To be honest, the oldest resort on the island is showing its age. The landscaping is negligible, the food serviceable at best, and from the outside the accommodations look more like barracks at a church camp than a luxe resort. Miked music blares like clockwork every day around sunset, and it's certainly noisier and more hyperactive than anything else on Grace Bay. But who cares? Even in the low season, the resort is packed with happy guests, filled to capacity when other resorts are half-full. Its appeal lies in its mix of nonstop activity and communal fun. Singles and couples come here to play in the sun—and this sprawling beachside campus has plenty of toys, including a flying trapeze.

The village-style cluster of basic two- and three-story accommodations contains comfortable, colorful rooms with twin or king-size beds, all designed with beachfront living in mind. The "all-inclusive" designation means that meals are included as well as most drinks—except the really good stuff, like champagne, certain premium liquors and wines, and canned and bottled drinks (be sure to check the fine print before you book). Among the three restaurants, **Grace Bay** serves breakfast, lunch, and dinner buffet style, and **Lucayan** offers a la carte meals and is open in the evening only (7:15–8:45pm; reservations required). Most meals are served at long, communal tables.

Grace Bay, Providenciales, Turks and Caicos, B.W.I. ✆ **800/258-2633** in the U.S., or 649/946-5500. Fax 649/946-5497. www.clubmed.us. 290 units. Winter $1,545–$1,722 per person weekly; off-season $1,300–$1,600 per person weekly. Rates are all-inclusive. AE, MC, V. No children 17 or under allowed. **Amenities:** 3 restaurants; 2 bars; open-air nightclub; basketball; flying trapeze; gym; outdoor pool; softball; 8 tennis courts (4 lit); trampoline; volleyball; watersports equipment (extensive); wellness center w/spa treatment rooms; Wi-Fi (free). *In room:* A/C, flatscreen TV, clock radio/CD player, hair dryer, minifridge.

The Gansevoort Turks + Caicos ★★★

The Gansevoort brand projects effortless chic. The resorts have an ingrained urbanity—no wonder, since the line's flagship hotel is the Gansevoort in Manhattan's Meatpacking District. Trendiness aside, these are superbly run hotels that dispense a healthy sense of warmth and hospitality. The Gansevoort Turks + Caicos has the hipness quotient down, but it also has a killer Grace Bay setting, and every one of the 91 rooms have ocean views to die for. The sun-blasted pool is a marvel in beachside feng shui; it's the nerve center of the resort, dotted with personal "floating islands." Rooms are smartly outfitted, with electric blackout blinds, LCD TVs, and cutting-edge kitchens; play "find the fridge" (it's camouflaged in the cabinetry). Bathrooms have glass-encased rain showers. And is it uncool to say that the big, deep tubs filled from a spigot high in the ceiling make us very happy? The "wow" factor hits the roof (literally) with four 345-sq.-m (3,700-sq.-ft.) three-bedroom penthouses—wraparound terraces, designer kitchens, personal concierge, a veritable VIP buffet. The **Bagatelle Bistrot** brings a sure, sophisticated touch to the island dining scene. But the breezy vibe is all Provo—especially at night, when the palms rustle in the trade winds and warm candlelight softens any urban edges.

Grace Bay, Providenciales, Turks and Caicos, B.W.I. ✆ **888/844-5986** in the U.S., or 649/941-7555. Fax 309/210-9091. www.gansevoortturksandcaicos.com. 91 units. Winter $575–$750 double, $950–$5,000 suite; off-season $350–$600 double, $600–$5,000 suite. Rates include continental breakfast. Children 11 and under stay free in parent's room. Extra person $100. AE, MC, V. **Amenities:** Restaurants; 2 bars; babysitting; children's program; concierge; fitness center; outdoor pool; room service; spa; watersports equipment (extensive). *In room:* A/C and ceiling fan, TV/DVD, CD player, hair dryer, kitchen (suites), kitchenettes (studios), MP3 docking station, room service; washer/dryer (suites), Wi-Fi (free).

Grace Bay Club ★★★ (Kids   This luxury boutique resort sets the bar for exemplary service in the TCI. Opened in 1993, it's one of the island's oldest hotels, but constant updating and refreshment by one of the finest management teams in the Caribbean underscores its commitment to excellence. You'll get plenty of pampering for your money—and a whopping repeat business proves they're doing things right. It doesn't hurt that the resort sits on the largest oceanfront acreage on Grace Bay (11 acres).

The hotel has accomplished the neat trick of creating three hotels in one (all with fabulous Grace Bay views): 1) The romantic **21-suite hotel** with its own pool, bar, and restaurant (Anacaona); 2) Four low-density villas containing **38 upscale, family-friendly condos,** positioned directly on the beach with their own pool and restaurant (Grill Rouge); and the newest addition, 3) **The Estate at Grace Bay Club,** 22 custom-designed ultraluxe oceanfront residences fronting a lap pool and a poolside bar/restaurant. The Estate's monumental 650-sq.-m (7,000-sq.-ft.) penthouse is utterly stunning, with four oceanfront bedrooms, a media room, and terraces for sublime views all around.

The Grace Bay Club personifies easy elegance, with a sun-burnished Mediterranean look and feel. Each of the villa accommodations has travertine-tile floors, custom-made imported furnishings, deep private patios, and superb oceanfront views. Each suite (except junior suites) and penthouse has its own state-of-the-art kitchen (granite countertops, stainless-steel appliances), washing machine, and dryer. The four 446-sq.-m (4,800-sq.-ft.) penthouses have outdoor Jacuzzis, among other luxuries. Spa specialists offer Euro-Asian treatments at the 465-sq.-m (5,000-sq.-ft.) **Spa Anani** (open 9am–6pm).

The hotel's main restaurant, **Anacaona** (see chapter 4), is one of Provo's top restaurants—but no kids 11 and under, please. Families can dine in the adjacent **Grill Rouge,** which offers casual alfresco dining with grilled seafood, panini, salads, and a kids' menu. The beachfront **Lounge,** with its Hamptons-style white-cushion seating and glowing fire pit, is one of the best spots on the island to have a cocktail and watch the sunset on Grace Bay; it now serves a tapas menu. But for sheer heat, check out the sexy **Infinity Bar,** which boasts the longest bar in the Caribbean, a sleek ribbon of black stone studded with glittering blue lights.

The children's program, **Kids' Town** (for kids 5–12), offers a full menu of half- or full-day excursions, including snorkeling, sailing, eco-activities, and kayaking; a dinnertime "campout" on the beach may include hot dogs and s'mores by a campfire.

1 Grace Bay Circle Rd. (P.O. Box 128), Providenciales, Turks and Caicos, B.W.I. *(C)* **800/946-5757** in the U.S., or 649/946-5050. Fax 649/946-5758. www.gracebay club.com. 59 units. Hotel: Winter $1,150 junior suite, $1,250–$1,750 1-bedroom suite, $2,100–$2,600 2-bedroom suite; off-season $650–$850 junior suite, $750–$1,300 1-bedroom suite, $1,250–$1,950 2-bedroom suite. Villas: Winter $950 junior suite, $1,750 1-bedroom suite, $2,100–$2,600 2-bedroom suite, $3,330 3-bedroom suite, $6,050–$8,500 penthouse; off-season $550–$700 junior suite, $1,050–$1,300 1-bedroom suite, $1,250–$1,950 2-bedroom suite, $1,950–$2,450 3-bedroom suite, $3,600–$6,550 penthouse. Estate: Winter $1,300–$10,000; off-season $800–$7,500. Ask about Christmas holiday rates. Extra person $150–$180. Rates include full breakfast. AE, DC, DISC, MC, V. Closed Sept. **Amenities:** 2 restaurants; 3 bars; bikes; fitness center; Jacuzzi; 2 outdoor pools; room service; spa; 2 lighted tennis courts; watersports equipment (extensive). *In room:* A/C, ceiling fan, TV w/DVD/CD player, hair dryer, kitchen (excluding junior suites), washer/dryer (excluding junior suites), Wi-Fi (free).

Point Grace ★★★   This boutique hotel opened in 2000 on a lyrical crescent of Grace Bay beachfront. In just 10 years, Point Grace has perfected an almost effortless graciousness and racked up one award after another, winning the World Travel Award for the Caribbean's Leading Boutique Hotel 4 years running. The motif is turn-of-the-20th-century British Colonial, and resort services and amenities are first rate, ranging from twice-daily maid service to midday sorbets on the beach. Don't expect the joint to be jumping: Even at its liveliest, generally during cocktail hour around the pool bar, this is a haven of quiet serenity. (Some say *too* quiet.) The **Thalasso Spa at Point Grace** (daily 9am–6pm) is a full-service on-site spa that offers spa treatments using sea mud and seaweed, among other delicacies, in whitewashed cottages open to the sea breezes—these are some of the best massages on the island.

The complex features exceptionally spacious one-, two-, three-, and four-bedroom suites and penthouses, furnished with Indonesian teak, and brightened by crisp white Frette linens; many are decorated with 200-year-old wall hangings from India. Hand-painted tile and mahogany grace the rooms, and each suite has a beautifully appointed kitchen and a washer/dryer.

Tucked away in a candlelit garden is **Grace's Cottage** (p. 91), perhaps the most romantic spot to dine on an island lousy with romantic restaurants.

Grace Bay (P.O. Box 700), Providenciales, Turks and Caicos, B.W.I. *(C)* **866/924-7223** in the U.S. or 649/946-5096. Fax 649/946-5097. www.pointgrace.com. 28 units. Winter $625–$675 cottage suites, $1,197 oceanfront suites, $1,517–$1,790 Atlantic suites, $2,048 Cotton Cay suite, $2,867 Big Cameron Cay suite; off-season $475–$525 cottage suites, $695–$915 oceanfront suites, $835–$1,365 Atlantic suites, $1,260–$1,560 Cotton Cay suite, $1,765–$2,185 Big Cameron Cay suite; ask about Christmas holiday rates. Rates include continental buffet breakfast; complimentary house cocktails and hors d'oeuvres at the pool bar 5–6pm; and airport transfers. AE, DISC, MC, V. **Amenities:** 2 restaurants; 2 bars; babysitting; bikes;

concierge; Internet (free); outdoor pool; room service; oceanfront spa; watersports equipment. *In room:* A/C, TV CD/DVD players, hair dryer, Internet (free), kitchen, washer/dryer, minibar.

The Regent Palms ★★★   Opened in early 2005, the Palms is one of Grace Bay's classiest lodgings, with some of the most handsomely appointed rooms on the island. But don't let its cool good looks intimidate you. Yes, the neo-Palladian centerpiece of the resort is referred to as "the Mansion"—but beneath that facade is a congenial Turks and Caicos ambience and a level of service that few resorts on the island can match. It even has kid-friendly amenities, such as the Conch Kritters Club, a daily activities program for kids 4 to 12. While the kids are off flying kites or hunting for lizards, you can relax in the gorgeous 2,323-sq.-m (25,005-sq.-ft.) **Regent Spa;** many of its 17 treatment rooms are in white-tented cabanas set in a classical arrangement around an outdoor reflecting pool.

The resort has two main gathering spots: the infinity pool and **Plunge,** the happening pool bar and lunch spot. Plunge has a sunken dining terrace and a swim-up bar—as you lie around the serpentine pool, you can check your e-mail and drink a toast to another tough day at the beach. The Mansion (fashioned after the theatrical Caribbean estates designed by Oliver Messel, the late British stage designer who also created Princess Margaret's "cottage" in Mustique) has a different feel entirely—more like a Tuscan villa overlooking a moonlit summer garden. The Mansion houses a clubby wood-paneled bar and the resort's main restaurant, **Parallel23,** which serves tropical-fusion cuisine from an open kitchen with a wood-burning oven; the restaurant's half-moon terrace fronts **Palm Place,** with shops on either side of a palm-lined courtyard.

Grace Bay Rd. (P.O. Box 681), Providenciales, Turks and Caicos, B.W.I. © **866/877-7256** or 649/946-8666. Christmas holiday reservations: © **305/532-7900** or info@thepalmstc.com only. Fax 649/946-5502. www.regentturksandcaicos.com or www.regenthotels.com/hotels/tcturks. 72 units. Winter $650–$675 double, $850–$1,400 1-bedroom suite, $1,675–$2,075 2-bedroom suite, $2,750 3-bedroom suite, $1,725–$3,075 penthouse; off-season $400–$475 double, $700–$825 1-bedroom suite, $1,150–$1,275 2-bedroom suite, $1,600–$1,725 3-bedroom suite, $1,425–$2,325 penthouse; inquire about Christmas holiday rates. Children 11 and under stay free in parent's room. Rates include continental buffet breakfast. AE, MC, V. **Amenities:** 2 restaurants; 2 bars; babysitting/nanny service; Conch Kritters Club; croquet pitch; fitness center (personal trainers available on request); Jacuzzi; infinity pool; room service; sauna; spa; Plexipave tennis courts; watersports equipment (extensive); yoga, Pilates, and meditation studio. *In room:* A/C, ceiling fan, TV (flat-panel LCD TVs in penthouses), hair dryer, full kitchens w/Viking appliances (in suites and penthouses), MP3 and MP3 docking station, minibar, Wi-Fi (free).

Seven Stars Resort ★ Kids   This luxury resort in the heart of Grace Bay has prevailed through financial difficulties and a changeover in ownership. Although it has dialed down its (considerable) expansion plans, it still has plenty to recommend it: a prime oceanfront location; spacious and beautifully appointed elegant one-, two-, and three-bedroom suites; and a palpable commitment to service. The entrance is lined with a classic colonnade of palms. The sprawling saltwater pool is the only heated pool on the island, great for toddlers. Kids also have a large playground to romp in. The **Deck bar** overlooking Grace Bay is a fun spot to drink in the sunset and dine on a tapas-style menu. Rooms are decorated in crisp British-Colonial style, with large windows, marble floors, and full or galley kitchens; many have wraparound terraces and four-poster beds. Bathrooms are filled with sunlight. We like the fact that the resort rates have become more competitive, and we like Seven Stars' community spirit: Even before it opened in early 2008, it gave Provo a holiday gift: a giant Christmas tree set in the middle of the traffic roundabout that fronts the property—the glittering colored lights were visible for miles.

Grace Bay, Providenciales, Turks and Caicos, B.W.I. ℂ **866/570-7777** or 649/941-7777. Fax 649/941-8601. www.sevenstarsresort.com. 120 units. Winter $650–$800 junior suite, $750–$900 1-bedroom suite, $1,500–$1,950 2-bedroom suite, $2,250–$3,500 3- and 4-bedroom suites, $1,000–$4,150 penthouse; off-season $350–$455 studio, $420–$455 1-bedroom suite, $868–$1,148 2-bedroom suite, $1,260–$1,690 3- and 4-bedroom suites, $560–$2,310 penthouse. Extra person 12 and over $50–$100 per night. Rates include continental breakfast. AE, MC, V. **Amenities:** 2 restaurants; pool lounge; babysitting/nanny service; children's playground; concierge; fitness center; outdoor pool; spa; 2 lighted tennis courts; watersports equipment (extensive); Wi-Fi (free, in pool, reception, and restaurant areas). *In room:* A/C, ceiling fans, flatscreen TV, DVD and CD players, hair dryer, Internet (free), full kitchen (in suites), galley kitchen (in studios).

The Somerset ★★★ Kids Is it just us, or is minimalist chic a bit of a tired cliché among beachside resorts these days? Maybe that's why the Somerset stands out, with its colorful Italianate style in striking contrast to all that cool monochrome. This 5-year-old resort looks and feels like an old-timer, in the best sense. The monumental neo-Tuscan architecture gives the place a solid feel, anchored by sweeping stone staircases and spraying fountains. Suites are masterfully appointed, with solid-wood French doors and a rich palette. If all this sounds prohibitively snooty, trust us: This is one of the friendliest, most relaxing spots on the island—this place hums along with maximum efficiency and minimum drama. It's smaller and quieter than its neighbor, the Regent Palms, and when the poolside grill closes at sunset, the pool is magically lit and palms sway in the night breeze, it's the very essence of serene tropical comfort.

The spacious rooms and suites are available in three accommodations categories: Estate, Stirling House, and Garden Cottage. The four blocks of ocean-view Estate suites comprise four full-floor suites per block (except the penthouse, which has two floors); each suite has a Viking grill and hot tub on its balcony. The Stirling House comprises 24 units, including both standard doubles (garden views) and suites (ocean views), and the 13 Garden Cottage units are duplexes with basement garages and garden views. Every suite has Viking equipment and appliances in the fully equipped kitchens, DVD/CD surround-sound Bose system (even on the balconies), travertine marble floors, and personal wine coolers. Each of the three penthouses has roof terraces with hot tubs and breathtaking 360-degree views. The resident restaurant, **O'Soleil,** has terrific food and service (see chapter 4), but we find the elegant white-on-white interior a little too frosty; we prefer to dine on one of the two handsome outdoor terraces. The lap pool stretches to the sea. Its reverse currents (and underwater audio) make this less a dip in a comforting bowl of blue than another experience altogether. An infinity pool near the edge of the dunes is a magnet for kids—and the poolside grill a great meeting-spot for families.

Grace Bay, Providenciales, Turks and Caicos, B.W.I. ✆ **877/887-5722** or 649/946-5900. www.thesomerset.com. 54 units. Winter $1,700–$4,000 Estate Villas, $500–$2,100 Stirling House suites and rooms, $350–$1,650 Garden Cottage suites; off-season $830–$3,000 Estate Villas, $275–$2,400 Stirling House suites and rooms, $500–$1,100 Garden Cottage suites. Rates include continental breakfast. Children 11 and under (maximum of 2) stay free in parent's room. Extra person $100. AE, DISC, MC, V. **Amenities:** 2 restaurants; pool bar; babysitting/nanny service; concierge; croquet pitch; infinity pool; room service; watersports equipment. *In room:* Zoned A/C, TV, hair dryer, full kitchen w/Viking appliances (in suites), MP3 docking station, private outdoor Jacuzzi (Estate suites), semiprivate elevators, Wi-Fi (free).

The Veranda ★★ (Kids)   Firmly in the expert hands of the Grace Bay Club management, this sprawling all-inclusive opened in February 2010 and already feels like a classic. Like the Grace Bay Club, it is divided into two main separate zones, the family-friendly West Village and the more adult-oriented East Village. The resort centerpiece, the Veranda House, has a more traditional feel, with tiered levels encircling a courtyard. The rest of the Veranda, set largely in two- and three-story buildings, looks more like a charming neighborhood in Key West or Nantucket than a posh resort: houses with gingerbread trim, rockers on wooden porches, and broad swathes of neatly trimmed green. Picket fences entwined with bougainvillea complete the picture. All of which is to say: There's nothing like it on Grace Bay. But step inside your room, and it's resort elegance all the way, in that English-cottage vein: beamed and wainscoted ceilings, plump bedding, and tastefully upholstered reproduction furnishings. (Note that most bathrooms have showers, not tubs.) The eight individual beachfront houses are the bomb: Wrapped in flower-draped white picket fencing, each cottage has around 370 sq. m (4,000 sq. ft.) of handsomely appointed living space and its own "front yard" with a plunge pool. The Veranda is a sprawling place, but intimate zones set around a lovely greensward or pool make it feel more like small-town neighborhoods. The main restaurant, the **Marin,** takes center stage facing the beach—this is the beating heart of the Veranda, with fire pits aglow at night, a bar illuminated in sultry blue lights, and a sec-ond-story **Sky Lounge** (with gazebo) where you can star-gaze while you sip.

Grace Bay, Providenciales, Turks and Caicos, B.W.I. (©) **877/945-5757** in the U.S. or 649/339-5050. Fax 649/946-5758. www.verandatco.com. 169 units. Call about winter rates; off-season $459 double, $636 1-bedroom suite, $885 2-bedroom suite, $1,062 3-bedroom suite. Rates are all-inclusive. AE, DISC, MC, V. **Amenities:** 2 restaurants; 2 bars; coffee/pastry shop; babysitting; bikes; concierge; fitness center; kids' program, playroom, and sandbox; 3 pools; spa; watersports equip-ment (extensive); Wii game room. *In room:* A/C, TV, hair dryer, full kitchen (except studios), Playstations, washer/dryers (except studios), Wi-Fi (free).

Expensive

Le Vele ★ This handsome boutique property sits on a picture-perfect stretch of Grace Bay beach. The resort contains only 22 units but is a great option for families. Each of the one-, two-, and three-bedroom condominium suites has room to spare, with oceanfront views, wraparound balconies, and full kitchens (excluding the studio suites). If you're looking for a quiet, intimate spot with a clean design steps away from the sea, this should fit the bill. It's not for everyone: The blocky white concrete gives the place a clinical feel. Although it doesn't have a restaurant or bar, you're minutes away from a number of fine Grace Bay options. Or you can take advantage of the suites' complete kitchens, with ovens, ranges, microwaves, stainless-steel fridges, and dishwashers.

Grace Bay, Providenciales, Turks and Caicos, B.W.I. (©) **888/272-4406** in the U.S. or 649/941-8800. www.levele.tc. 22 units. Winter $474 double, $664 1-bedroom suite, $949 2-bedroom suite, $1,360 3-bedroom suite; off-season $348 double, $474 1-bedroom suite, $696 2-bedroom suite, $1,044 3-bedroom suite. Extra per-son $60 per night. Rates include continental breakfast delivered to your suite. AE, DISC, MC, V. **Amenities:** Babysitting; bikes; fitness center; concierge/excursion desk; infinity pool; watersports equipment. *In room:* A/C, TV/DVD/CD, full kitchens, hair dryer, washer/dryers (excluding studio suites), Wi-Fi (free).

Ocean Club Resorts ★ (Kids) These two condo-hotel complexes are within a mile of one another, both with prime oceanfront acreage on Grace Bay. The original, **Ocean Club East,** lies across from the Provo Golf Club, spread across a 3-hectare (7½-acre) piece of land-scaped property. It shares amenities with its newer sister resort, **Ocean Club West,** and a complimentary shuttle runs between the two. Both comprise a low-lying series of buildings surrounding gardens and a courtyard.

Both resorts have 86 suites, among them studio suites, junior suites, and one-, two-, or three-bedroom deluxe suites—many with ocean views and fully equipped kitchens (studios have kitchenettes only). (The main difference between East and West is that only Ocean Club East offers studio deluxe and one-bedroom beachfront suites.) Except for the studio suites (the cheapest rental), accommodations are spacious and comfortable, with large screened balconies. The decor is light, bright, and pleasant if not particularly exciting—but on a slice of beach this delicious, who's spending much time in their room?

With their large suite size and fully appointed kitchens, these resorts are family-vacation favorites. Both resorts have a Kids Clubhouse, a day camp for children 3½ and up from 9:30am to 1pm daily.

The resorts' newest restaurant, **Opus,** located at Ocean Club East in the Ocean Club Plaza, offers upscale Continental dining. Also in the plaza is an annex for Art Pickering's Provo Turtle Divers Ltd. (see "Scuba Diving & Snorkeling," in chapter 5). There's also a daily shuttle-bus service for dining in the evenings and a part-time shuttle bus for daytime shopping, both for a small fee. A complimentary shuttle runs between the resorts.

Grace Bay Beach (P.O. Box 240), Providenciales, Turks and Caicos, B.W.I. ℂ **800 457-8787** in the U.S. or 649/946-5880. Fax 649/946-5845. www.oceanclubresorts. com. 186 units. Winter $270–$280 studio suite, $310–$410 junior suite, $385–$575 1-bedroom suite, $510–$670 2-bedroom suite, $800–$915 3-bedroom suite; off-season $180–$195 studio suite, $205–$280 junior suite, $265–$395 1-bedroom suite, $3855–$495 2-bedroom suite, $550–$695 3-bedroom suite. Call about Christmas holiday rates. Children 11 and under stay free in parent's room. AE, DISC, MC, V. **Amenities:** 3 restaurants (Seaside Café is in Ocean Club West); 3 bars; babysitting; bikes; concierge; convenience store; dive shop; fitness room; 3 freshwater pools; 3 lighted tennis courts; watersports equipment (extensive). In room: A/C, ceiling fan, TV/VCR, kitchen (kitchenettes in studios), hair dryer, washer/dryer (excluding studios), Wi-Fi (free).

The Regent Grand ★ Occupying a central spot on Grace Bay oceanfront, this all-suites resort is an impressive property of classical design, with a breathtaking centerpiece of a pool (the biggest in the TCI!), a tennis court, and a shopping-and-restaurant complex next door in Regent Village. The suites are large and comfortably furnished and have everything you need—including fully equipped kitchens—but layouts are a little uninspired. But that's okay, since you'll have every amenity under the sun and a swell piece of beachfront to play on.

Grace Bay Rd. (P.O. Box 124), Providenciales, Turks and Caicos, B.W.I. ℂ **877/537-3314** or 649/941-7770. Fax: 649/941-7771. www.theregentgrandresort.com. 54 units. Winter $489 double, $794–$1,358 1-bedroom suite, $1,058–$1,886 2-bedroom suite, $2,185–$2,875 3-bedroom suite; off-season $3,455 double, $656–$1,047 1-bedroom suite, $759–$1,541 2-bedroom suite, $1,840–$2,300 3-bedroom suite, $1,425–$2,325 penthouse; inquire about Christmas holiday rates. Extra person $50 ($80 holidays). Children 11 and under stay free in parent's room. Rates include continental breakfast delivered to the suite and airport transfers. AE, MC, V. **Amenities:** 2 restaurants; 2 bars; babysitting; bikes; fitness center; pool; spa; room service; 2 lighted tennis courts; watersports equipment (extensive). *In room:* A/C, ceiling fan, TV/DVD, hair dryer, full kitchens, Wi-Fi (free).

Royal West Indies Resort ★ (Kids) This is one of the most reliable, well-managed condo-hotel resorts along Grace Bay, offering family-friendly lodging and a prime location on one of the best sections of beach, between the Grandview on Grace Bay and Club Med. Surrounding the property are well-manicured gardens, the centerpiece of which is a large pool enveloped in tropical foliage. It's a pretty big place, with 99 units, but rooms are situated in intimate groupings of low-rise buildings spread out over the spacious property. Guests have a choice of oceanfront, oceanview, studio, or garden-view one- and two-bedroom suites. Suites are large and have balconies or patios and good-size kitchenettes. The interiors have been very nicely refurbished with comfortable, well-maintained furnishings and good linens. Even if you're not a guest, we strongly recommend a meal at **Mango Reef** (see chapter 4), the casual poolside restaurant with consistently fresh, delicious food.

Grace Bay (P.O. Box 482), Providenciales, Turks and Caicos, B.W.I. © **800/332-4203** in the U.S. or 649/946-5004. Fax 649/946-5008. www.royalwestindies.com. 99 units. Winter $285–$425 studio, $385–$625 1-bedroom suite, $525–$795 2-bedroom suite; off-season $225–$345 studio, $275–$445 1-bedroom suite, $485–$545 2-bedroom suite. Extra person 13 or over $35 per night. Children 12 and under stay free in parent's room. AE, DISC, MC, V. **Amenities:** Restaurant; bar; babysitting; bikes; Jacuzzi; 2 outdoor pools; watersports equipment (extensive); Wi-Fi (free, in lobby and hot spot). *In room:* A/C, ceiling fan, TV, hair dryer, kitchen, washer/dryer.

The Sands at Grace Bay ★★ (Kids) The Sands has always been a popular choice on Grace Bay, but a top-notch refurbishment in 2008—including the construction of an elegant new freestanding lobby—put it in another league altogether. This sprawling all-suites condo resort is set on a prime stretch of Grace Bay Beach. Suites have been tastefully and luxuriously updated, with granite countertops, marble sinks, and fine linens. The manicured gardens and pools are impeccably maintained—this is one well-managed property. Choose from studio, one-bedroom, two-bedroom, or three-bedroom suites— each of which is fully appointed, with screened terraces. The suites also have full kitchens (studios have kitchenettes) and washer/ dryers—great for family stays. The Sands is the site of one of the island's most popular beachfront restaurants, **Hemingway's** (p. 94), and the **Spa Tropique at the Sands.** Ask about the bed-and-breakfast options.

Grace Bay, Providenciales, Turks and Caicos, B.W.I. ☎ **877/777-2637** in the U.S. or 649/946-5199. Fax 649/946-5198. www.thesandstc.com. 116 units. Winter $285–$460 studio, $460–$710 1-bedroom suite, $560–$710 2-bedroom suite, $800–$1,200 3-bedroom suite; off-season $185–$330 studio, $330–$530 1-bedroom suite, $430–$580 2-bedroom suite, $530–$830 3-bedroom suite. Children 11 and under stay free in parent's suite (maximum of 2). AE, DISC, MC, V. **Amenities:** Restaurant; bar; babysitting; bikes; dive shop; fitness center; Jacuzzi; 3 outdoor pools; supermarket shuttle ($8 per person round-trip); spa services; tennis court; watersports equipment (extensive). *In room:* A/C, ceiling fan, TV, hair dryer, full kitchen (kitchenette in studios), washer/dryer, Wi-Fi (free).

Turks & Caicos Club ★ (Finds)

This quiet and peaceful Lower Bight pioneer has only 21 suites (one- and two-bedroom), each with four-poster beds, a gourmet kitchen, and its own big, private porch. You can choose from oceanfront, with sumptuous views of Grace Bay beach, or poolside (with lower rates). The rooms are nicely appointed (the kitchens have state-of-the-art KitchenAid appliances), but the porches make it special. A talented chef is on board at the in-house restaurant, **Simba ★**; the island-style conch chowder is a fiery masterpiece.

Grace Bay (P.O. Box 687), Providenciales, Turks and Caicos, B.W.I. ☎ **649/946-5800**. Fax 649/946-5858. www.turksandcaicosclub.com. 21 units. Winter $445–$595 1-bedroom suite, $1,095 2-bedroom suite; summer $325–$495 1-bedroom suite, $655–$845 2-bedroom suite. Rates include continental breakfast. AE, MC, V. **Amenities:** Restaurant; pool bar; fitness room; room service; watersports equipment (extensive). *In room:* A/C, TV/VCR/DVD, iPod speakers, hair dryer, kitchen, Wi-Fi (free).

Villa Renaissance ★★ (Finds)

This little gem lies on a central stretch of Grace Bay oceanfront. It has a lovely reception area (the Pavilion), a large, gorgeous mosaic pool, and in the **Teona Spa** a full-service spa on-site. A new restaurant, the **Vix**, recently opened at nearby sister property Regent Grand (as part of the Regent Village complex) and serves fresh seafood and international fare (closed Sun). The classical architecture (much like an Italian villa) is beautiful, and the rooms are comfortable and nicely outfitted.

Grace Bay (P.O. Box 592), Providenciales, Turks and Caicos, B.W.I. ☎ **877/285-8764** in the U.S. or 649/941-5300. Fax 649/941-5340. www.villarenaissance.com. 36 units. Winter $600–$870 1-bedroom suite, $755–$1,140 2-bedroom suite, $1,525 3-bedroom suite, $1,920 penthouse; off-season $445–$770 1-bedroom suite, $645–$900 2-bedroom suite, $1,085 3-bedroom suite, $1,325 penthouse. Extra person 13 or over $85 per night. Rates include continental breakfast. AE, DISC, MC, V. **Amenities:** Pool bar; babysitting; bikes; concierge; fitness center; spa; lighted tennis courts; watersports equipment; Wi-Fi (free, in courtyard/pool area). *In room:* A/C, TV/DVD, fridge, hair dryer, kitchen.

The West Bay Club ★★ (Value)

For those to whom a prime location and top-notch accommodations mean more than having a splashy destination restaurant, state-of-the-art spa, or sizzling lounge scene, the West Bay Club represents fantastic value on beachfront Grace Bay. Opened in 2009, this Lower Bight property was designed by Simon Wood, the celebrated architect also responsible for the Gansevoort next door. This boutique resort has a decidedly more laidback feel than its neighbor to the west, but its rooms share equally luxurious trappings. The West Bay Club has some of the biggest suites on Grace Bay, outfitted to the heavens. Suites are sheathed in marble floors with huge (46 in.) flat-panel TVs, DVD/CD surround-sound Bose theater systems, MP3 docks, full kitchens with stainless-steel appliances and granite countertops, oceanfront terraces, and a surplus of closet space. Particularly good value are the multi-bedroom suites and the glamorous penthouses, the largest of which are 350 sq. m (3,800 sq. ft.), with Grace Bay views that go on forever. By design, the hotel amenities are modest—the pool is smallish, the modest restaurant has only nine tables (but the food is fresh and delicious!; see chapter 4), and the bar is just a smattering of stools. Here the emphasis is firmly on luxe rooms and a prime location along Grace Bay. The property was smartly conceived and built to last—an underground bunker contains all the inner workings, including a complete commercial laundry, a cistern, and a waste-management system. It all purrs along with the expert guidance of the warm and unpretentious management, a husband-and-wife team offering mom-and-pop luxe.

Lower Bight Rd., Grace Bay, Providenciales, Turks and Caicos, B.W.I. © 866/607-4156 in the U.S. or 649/946-8550. Fax 649/946-3722. www.thewestbayclub.com. 46 units. Winter $300 studio, $495–$521 1-bedroom suite, $595–$695 2-bedroom suite, $975 3-bedroom suite, $1,100–$1,265 penthouse; off-season $235 studio, $400–$450 1-bedroom suite, $500–$595 2-bedroom suite, $690 3-bedroom suite, $795–$900 penthouse. Extra person $75 per night. Rates include European breakfast. AE, DISC, MC, V. **Amenities:** Restaurant; bar; babysitting; bikes; concierge; fitness center; pool; room service; spa; watersports equipment. *In room:* A/C, ceiling fan, TV, DVD/CD, hair dryer, kitchen (except studios), MP3 docking station, washer/dryer (except studios), Wi-Fi (free).

Moderate

The Alexandra ★ Ⓥalue   This sprawling all-suites resort directly on Grace Bay is a work in progress, with four buildings completed and one to go. The Alexandra has a great location and big plans for a full-tilt resort experience, including a casino, ice-cream parlor, and more. Currently, it features a big, beautiful pool with a swim-up bar, a spa, a fitness center, the **Sunset Dining Deck** overlooking Grace Bay, and a full-service restaurant, the **Orchid,** which serves local and Continental cuisine. It represents good value, especially if you want to be on Grace Bay and don't want to spend a fortune to do so. The locally owned Alexandra currently has 170 suites, but when the last building is finished, it will add 50 more. You can choose from studios all the way up to four-bedroom suites (lockouts) in three different categories: superior luxury (right on the ocean), luxury (oceanfront views), and deluxe (garden and partial ocean views). The suites are smallish but pleasant enough, and all but the studios have full kitchens (studios have kitchenettes), but they don't approach the luxe factor of places like the Regent Palms, right next door. Still, the Alexandra is currently a good-value lodging and welcomes families.

Princess Dr., Grace Bay, Providenciales, Turks and Caicos, B.W.I. ✆ **800/704-9424** in the U.S. or 649/946-5807. Fax 649/946-4686. www.alexandraresort.com. 220 units. Winter $285–$660 deluxe suites, $480–$1,560 luxury suites; off-season $215–$540 deluxe suites, $360–$1,320 luxury suites. Rates include 10% onsite restaurant discount. AE, MC, V. **Amenities:** Restaurant; grill/bar; ice-cream shop; basketball; fitness center; outdoor pool and kids' pool; room service; spa; 2 lighted tennis courts; volleyball; watersports equipment (extensive). *In room:* A/C, ceiling fan, TV/DVD (flatscreen in luxury suites), full kitchen (kitchenette in studios), hair dryer, washer/dryer (most suites), Wi-Fi (free).

Coral Gardens/Reef Residences on Grace Bay ⓥalue This

Grace Bay resort fronts one of the beach's top snorkeling and diving spots on Bight Reef in the Princess Alexandra National Park. The Reef Residences lies behind Coral Gardens and has no ocean views—plus, the two places have different management teams. Most, if not all, of the units are condos, with each unit privately owned. Suites are large (full kitchens and even walk-in closets in some) and deep, with expansive balconies. Excellent snorkeling and diving opportunities lie literally right out your door; the dive operator **Caicos Adventures** has a shop onsite and offers scuba courses, snorkeling tours, and complimentary snorkeling equipment. A new restaurant, **Somewhere Café & Lounge,** serves breakfast, lunch, and dinner with a Tex-Mex bent.

Lower Bight Road, Grace Bay (P.O. Box 281), Providenciales, Turks and Caicos, B.W.I. ✆ **800/532-8536** in the U.S. or 649/941-3713. Fax 649/941-5171. www.coralgardens. com. 30 units. Winter $249 garden double, $399–$449 1-bedroom oceanfront suite, $499–$599 2-bedroom oceanfront suite, $559–$750 penthouse; off-season $199 garden double, $300–$349 1-bedroom oceanfront suite, $400–$500 2-bedroom oceanfront suite, $459–$599 penthouse. Extra person 10 years or older $30 a night. Children 9 and under stay free in parent's room. Rates include full breakfast. AE, DISC, MC, V. **Amenities:** 1 restaurant; 1 bar; babysitting; bikes; dive and snorkel shop; fitness center; 2 outdoor pools; spa; watersports equipment (extensive). *In room:* A/C, TV, CD and DVD players, full kitchen, hair dryer, washer/dryer (in penthouses and Ocean Grand suites), Wi-Fi (free).

Inexpensive

Caribbean Paradise Inn ⓥalue This intimate, cozy inn is a real find, considering that it's only a 2-minute walk from lovely Grace Bay Beach *and* the low, low rates include a breakfast buffet. It has also been a hub of activity since chef Paul Newman moved the popular restaurant **Coyaba** from its longtime location in Coral Gardens to the adjoining bar/patio area; even though the restaurant is run independently from the inn, the lively dining scene gives the place a jolt of electricity. Two stories of rooms overlook the pool and a nice tropical courtyard. Combination bedrooms and living areas, with a patio or balcony, the rooms have been nicely refreshed, with tile floors and a king or two full beds. The small bathrooms have showers only. The owner, Jean Luc Bohic, is extremely personable.

Grace Bay (P.O. Box 673), Providenciales, Turks and Caicos, B.W.I. © **877/946-5020** in the U.S. or 649/946-5020. Fax 649/946-5022. www.caribbean-paradise-inn.com. 17 units. Winter $147–$168 double; off-season $118–$135 double. Extra person $35. Children 4 and under stay free in parent's room. Rates include buffet breakfast. MC, V. **Amenities:** Bar; babysitting; outdoor freshwater pool; watersports. *In room:* A/C, ceiling fan, TV, fridge/minibar, hair dryer, Wi-Fi ($10/day)

Comfort Suites (Value) This is the first franchise hotel to open on Provo and for central location alone represents great value. The nicely refurbished suites are more than suitable, and the hospitality provided by the staff is exceptional. The handsomely landscaped property is a 2-minute walk to the beach, restaurants, and shops. Guests stay here in one of the spacious junior suites, with either a king-size or two double beds, or in a suite with a balcony. Accommodations are spread across two three-floor structures, enveloping a large swimming pool, pool bar, and a courtyard.

Grace Bay Rd. (P.O. Box 590), Providenciales, Turks and Caicos, B.W.I. © **888/678-3483** in the U.S. or 649/946-8888. Fax 649/946-5444. www.comfortsuitestci.com. 100 units. Winter $165–$185 suite; off-season $150–$175 suite. Rates include breakfast. Children 15 and under stay free in parent's room. Extra person $30. AE, DISC, MC, V. **Amenities:** Bar; babysitting; outdoor pool. *In room:* A/C, TV, hair dryer, Wi-Fi (free).

Sibonné Beach Hotel ★ (Value) One of the first lodgings constructed on the fabulous sands of Grace Bay Beach, this hotel is a fantastic value, as long as you don't expect a huge laundry list of resort amenities (and you don't expect the staff to shower you with love). What it does have is a laid-back, informal vibe; alluring courtyard gardens; and knockout Grace Bay views. It's considerably more charming and personable than any chain-style hotel, with comfortable rooms done up in a light, breezy decor. For a stupendous deal on Grace Bay, book the one-bedroom upstairs apartment, detached from the actual hotel. It has a full kitchen, with pots, pans, plates, the works; a separate living room; a big, comfortable bed; and two ocean-front patios, one screened, one open—you'll feel as if you have your own sunny beachfront cottage within spitting distance of the million-dollar sands of the Regent Palms. On-site is the **Bay Bistro,** a casual beachside restaurant offering exceptional breakfast, lunch, and dinner fare; and **Junior's Bar,** whose bartender extraordinaire, Junior Brown, is considered one of the most creative mixologists on island. *Note:* Sibonné does not accept children 12 and under in the winter or holiday season.

Grace Bay (P.O. Box 144), Providenciales, Turks and Caicos, B.W.I. © **800/528-1905** in the U.S. or 649/946-5547. Fax 649/946-5770. www.sibonne.com. 29 units. Winter $125–$235 double, $375 apt; off-season $110–$205 double, $285 apt. Rates include continental breakfast. Extra person $45; children 11 and under $35 (no children 12 and under in winter or holiday season). AE, MC, V. **Amenities:** Restaurant; bar; outdoor pool. *In room:* A/C, ceiling fan, TV, fridge, hair dryer, Wi-Fi (free).

NORTHWEST POINT

Those in the know say that this section of Provo represents the future of the country's hospitality industry. Unlike Grace Bay's long, developable stretch of beach, the beaches at the Northwest Point are serendipitous little coves with pockets of powdery white sand and turquoise seas. As the area develops, the plan is to create a lot of greenbelted area and ensure no structure over three stories tall is built. The waters along the Northwest Point are part of the **Northwest Point Marine National Park,** a protected 8km-long (5-mile) reef system that features some of the world's top wall and reef diving.

Currently the Northwest Point has only two accommodations: Amanyara (see below), and the **Northwest Point Resort** condominium hotel (www.northwestpointresort.com). To reach either, you travel through the Blue Hills neighborhood, where beachfront shacks dish out fresh conch dishes, good music, and a sunny barefoot vibe (see "Dining Da Blue Hills," in chapter 4).

Amanyara ★★★ The first Amanresorts property in the West Indies was such a big deal when it opened in early 2006 that *Travel + Leisure* magazine devoted an entire cover article to it. This is unfussy luxury, with Amanresorts' trademark purity of form, integrity of materials, and commitment to eco-principles. The prices are heartstopping, but no detail has been left to chance. Classically aligned main resort buildings appear to float on the surrounding reflecting pools. The bar has a golden imported-wood ceiling that soars toward the sunlight. The infinity pool, fashioned of speckled black Indonesian lava, is lorded over by linen-wrapped sofa beds.

The 40 individual pavilions are stand-alone houses, and utterly private; a few have ocean views. Wraparound patios are enveloped in native scrub brush, sea grape, and sea ox-eye daisies. It's very earthbound, if not for the exceptional gadgets: Flip open your laptop and go online, groove to the surround-sound Bose system, or switch on the flatscreen TV as you soak in the freestanding bathtub.

The **Restaurant** serves a menu with Asian-Mediterranean influences either inside or on a candlelit patio; the **Beach Club** serves lunch and afternoon meals. The smiling resort staff love children; management is happy to provide not only cribs and nannies, but Diaper Champs, toddler stools, and training potties—the kitchen even makes homemade baby food! But in my experience, crying babies and unruly toddlers do not a happy Amanyara clientele make—and who can blame them? They've come here for stress-free R&R and deeply pampered serenity. (*Too* much serenity for some; more than one Grace Bay hotelier reported weekly check-ins from Amanyara guests going buggy with all that peace and quiet.).

The serenity is tied to location as well: The resort lies on the island's northwest shore, a pretty isolated spot that is reached by traveling a winding two-lane road some 25 minutes from the airport. If you're keen on exploring the island, know that you're a good 30- to 40-minute drive from the action in Provo.

Note that the resort has three privately owned three-, four-, and five-bedroom villas. Each villa is centered on its own infinity pool and has a personal cook and housekeeper (winter $5,600–$13,950; off-season $4,300–$11,700).

Northwest Point, Providenciales, Turks and Caicos, B.W.I. ☎ **866/941-8133** or 649/941-8133. Fax 649/941-8132. www.amanyara.com. 40 private pavilions. Winter $1,550–$2,150; off-season $1,200–$1,800; ask about Christmas holiday rates. Rates include private airport transfers, minibar (except spirits), in-room Internet access, and all telephone calls. Children 12 and under stay free in parent's pavilion. AE, MC, V. **Amenities:** 2 restaurants; bar/lounge; afternoon tea; babysitting; fitness center; outdoor pool; Serenity Villa (spa, beauty services, and yoga classes); screening room; 2 clay tennis courts; watersports equipment. *In room:* A/C, TV, DVD/CD player, hair dryer, minibar/fridge, Wi-Fi (free).

TURTLE COVE

The **Queen Angel Resort,** a 56-unit condo hotel that lies across from Turtle Cove and is a 5-minute walk from the beach, is an attractive and reasonably priced option in both high and low seasons. It features suites with full kitchens and has a nicely landscaped pool (☎ **649/ 941-7907;** www.queenangelresort.com; year-round $130–$150 double, $150–$225 one-bedroom suite, $225–$250).

Turtle Cove Inn Ⓥalue You'll be hard-pressed to find a better lodging deal in Provo than this two-story hotel, built in a U shape around a freshwater swimming pool amid tropical vegetation. It's a longtime favorite with divers and boaters. It's a good choice for vacationers on a budget (it's the well-run sister inn to Sibonné, the charming and equally well-run Grace Bay oceanfront resort). A few feet away, boats dock directly at the hotel's pier, which juts into Seller's Pond amid the many yachts floating at anchor. Each bedroom is clean and simply but adequately furnished, with views over either the pool or the marina. Turtle Cove has a number of fun, funky restaurants.

Turtle Cove Marina, Suzie Turn Rd. (P.O. Box 131), Providenciales, Turks and Caicos, B.W.I. © **800/887-0477** in the U.S. or 649/946-4203. Fax 649/946-4141. www. turtlecoveinn.com. 28 units. Winter $105–$140 double, $140 marina-view apt; off-season $80–$100 double, $130 marina-view apt. Children 12 and under stay free in parent's room. AE, MC, V. **Amenities:** Restaurant; bar; outdoor pool; babysitting. *In room:* A/C, ceiling fan, TV, fridge, Wi-Fi (free).

2 CAICOS CAYS

PARROT CAY

Parrot Cay ★★★ This luxury resort is a favored retreat of celebrities, but you don't have to be a movie star to enjoy Parrot Cay's warm embrace and high service standards—standards that are impeccably and rigorously maintained. Parrot Cay defines excellence. More important, our 4-year-old wants to move here. To that we say "Amen!"—Parrot Cay is a wonderful place to be.

The resort lies on an isolated and private 400-hectare (988-acre) island—reputedly a former pirate's lair—with a powdery white-sand beach. The compound features 10 white colonial-style buildings, each with a terra-cotta-tile roof. Rooms have louvered doors that open onto terraces or verandas, oyster-white walls with tongue-and-groove paneling, and mosquito netting over four-poster beds. The spacious tiled bathrooms are beautifully appointed with a big tub and a shower and the spa's Invigorate toiletries. The best units are the roomy, handsome beach houses and villas, which offer utter privacy and direct access to the beach. Beach houses have plunge pools and hardwood verandas. Beach villas (one to three bedrooms) are even roomier, with swimming pools and kitchenettes.

Many come to Parrot Cay for the sublime treatments in the **COMO Shambhala** holistic spa, the finest spa in the Caribbean, which encompasses a wood pavilion wrapped in a sea of glass that looks out over the marsh wetlands. In addition, the resort has an infinity pool and access to scuba diving, Hobie Cats, snorkeling, kayaks, and water-skiing. Kids' activities are available as well.

During the Christmas holidays and spring breaks, this celeb magnet becomes a big softie for kids, when families come for long stays and the shallow waters are seeded with colorful conch shells for kids' treasure hunts and messages in bottles appear on the beach.

The **Terrace** restaurant, in the resort's main building, serves breakfast and dinner, specializing in Mediterranean cuisine. Lunch and dinner are served in **Lotus,** a romantic torch-lit poolside restaurant with Southeast Asian–inspired cuisine (along with regular-Joe lunch favorites like hamburgers); both restaurants offer a healthful Shambhala spa menu. With all this wonderfulness going on, is it curmudgeonly of me to lodge a complaint? The only drawback here is that you're limited to the resort's two restaurants, which may not match up to the best offerings on Grace Bay—Lotus's Asian fusion cuisine doesn't always hit the mark. On the other hand, the food is always ultrafresh and impeccably sourced, and the bountiful breakfasts at the Terrace were among the best we had in Provo.

Parrot Cay (P.O. Box 164), Providenciales, Turks and Caicos, B.W.I. ⓒ 866/388-0036 in the U.S. or 649/946-7788. Fax 649/946-7789. www.parrotcay.com or http://parrotcay.como.bz. 60 units. Winter $938–$1,180 double, $1,997 1-bedroom suite, $3,509 1-bedroom beach house, $4,235–$7,563 beach villa; off-season $696–$1,029 double, $1,210–$1,634 1-bedroom suite, $2,481–$2,783 1-bedroom beach house, $3,146–$5,808 beach villa. Ask about Christmas holiday rates. Extra person 13 and over $210. Rates include full American breakfast and return airport transfers by car and hotel boat (commercially scheduled flights only). AE, MC, V. Reached by a 30-min. private boat ride north from Provo, leaving from Leeward Marina. **Amenities:** 2 restaurants; 2 bars; babysitting; fitness center; Jacuzzi; nature trail; room service; outdoor pool; sauna; spa; 2 tennis courts; watersports equipment (extensive). *In room:* A/C, ceiling fan, TV/DVD, radio/CD player, hair dryer, kitchenette (in some), minibar, Wi-Fi (free).

PINE CAY

The Meridian Club ★★ Don't expect luxury of the marble-floors or gilded-chandeliers variety—this is what is lovingly referred to as "barefoot elegance"—and be prepared to live without television, radio, and even air-conditioning. This is the high life of an entirely different sort, the kind where you and a lucky few others are willing castaways on a private island paradise. The Meridian Club is one of the TCI pioneers, having been established on 324-hectare (800-acre) Pine Cay way back in 1973. To get here, you either take a 30-minute boat ride from Provo or fly in to the tiny island airstrip used by Meridian Club guests and the island's homeowners. The island has no cars: To get around, you either hoof it or, if you're in a hurry, tool around in an electric golf cart. The beach in front of the resort is simply extraordinary, and sand dollars float up without fail on the tawny sands of Sand Dollar Point, mere yards away. The snorkeling in the coral gardens offshore is satisfyingly good. The meals—included in the rates—are hearty, nutritious, plentiful, and insanely tasty—with an emphasis on fresh seafood. If you require still more privacy, opt for the Sand Dollar Cottage, a six-sided "hut" with a flagstone floor and lots of light from the louvered windows, set apart from the other rooms and almost directly on the beach.

It's all wonderful, and each of the nicely outfitted, comfortable rooms has a spacious bathroom, screened-in porch, and patio with a decadent outdoor shower. Check the resort website for the latest packages and special offers. *Note:* Children 11 and under are only allowed as guests in the months of June and July.

Pine Cay, Providenciales, Turks and Caicos, B.W.I. © **866/746-3229** in the U.S. or 649/941-7011. Fax 649/941-7010. www.meridianclub.com. E-mail reservations to reservations@meridianclub.com. 12 units. Winter $1,055–$1,130 club rooms, $1,205–$1,280 Sand Dollar Cottage; off-season $765–$850 club room, $915–$1,000 Sand Dollar Cottage. Rates include all meals, afternoon tea, and round-trip airport transfers by car and hotel boat; alcoholic beverages not included. Extra person $175 per night. AE, DISC, MC, V. Reached by a 30-min. private boat ride north from Provo, leaving from Leeward Marina. Closed Aug 1–Oct 31. **Amenities:** Restaurant; bar; bikes; commissary; outdoor pool; spa services; tennis court; watersports equipment (extensive); Wi-Fi (in computer room only; free). *In room:* Ceiling fan, hair dryer.

3 NORTH CAICOS

Rural, green, and charmingly slow-paced, North Caicos has its share of gorgeous powdery-sand beaches, which at press time you could enjoy with a few other lucky souls during stays at modest, moderately priced lodgings. The bones of the unfinished **Royal Reef Resort** overlook uninhabited Sandy Point, its completion still up in the air at press time.

Bottle Creek Lodge   The Bottle Creek Lodge offers three comfortable, colorful cottages, each with fully equipped kitchenettes and nice views of Bottle Creek. One, the Seashell Bungalow, has two bedrooms, 1½ bathrooms, and a deck. The lodge restaurant serves continental breakfast as well as lunch and dinner, and is open from August through March. The lodge is bountifully equipped with big-kid toys (sea kayaks, windsurf boards, bikes, and snorkeling equipment) and is happy to arrange adventure trips on North Caicos and to nearby islands. Ask about fishing/lodging packages. Calls to the U.S. and Canada are free from the courtesy phone in the lodge.

Belmont, North Caicos, Turks and Caicos, B.W.I. **703/297-8224.** www.bottlecreek lodge.com. 3 units. Cottages May 15–Nov 14 $155–$180 per night; Nov 15–May 14 $205–$240 per night. MC, V. **Amenities:** Restaurant; bar; bikes; watersports equipment (extensive). *In room:* A/C (for fee in 2 units), full kitchenettes, Wi-Fi (free).

Hollywood Beach Suites   This is a real getaway and almost feels like camping out, except you have a fully equipped suite in which to park your bones, and a kitchen (and outdoor barbecue grill) to cook the day's catch (supplied by local fishermen if you request it in advance). You can also have a local cook prepare a real island meal for you; just ask the helpful manager. Bikes, kayaks, and snorkeling equipment are available for guest use, but you may be tempted to spend your time simply daydreaming in a hammock on the tranquil beach (or on the deck overlooking the water) just steps away from the suites.

Hollywood Beach Dr., Whitby, North Caicos, Turks and Caicos, B.W.I. ℂ **800/551-2256** in the U.S. or 649/231-1020. Fax 702/973-6659. www.hollywoodbeachsuites. com. 4 units. Winter $356 1-bedroom suite; off-season $253 1-bedroom suite. AE, MC, V. **Amenities:** Bikes; grill; watersports equipment. *In room:* A/C, ceiling fan, TV/DVD/VCR, fully equipped kitchens, hair dryer, washer/dryer, no phones, Wi-Fi (free).

Pelican Beach Hotel This small, pleasant guesthouse feels as if it's from another era, with a pitched timbered ceiling and wood paneling; the only thing missing is the ticking of a grandfather clock. Outside, casuarina pines shade a conch-strewn beach lapped by turquoise seas. Owners Clifford and Susie Gardiner call this place the "unresort" and have created a mellow homey vibe, which Susie's delicious home cooking only serves to underscore. The rooms are plain but comfortable. You can snorkel nearby, have the Gardiners arrange a boat excursion or island tour, or join the bird-watchers who flock here to see pink flamingos and ospreys. Or relax and enjoy the peace and quiet. As they like to say here at Pelican Beach: "Sometimes, you'll find, doing nothing is wonderful."

Pelican Beach, North Caicos, Turks and Caicos, B.W.I. ℂ **649/946-7112.** www.pelicanbeach.tc. 16 units. Dec 20–Apr 19 $265 double with meals, $200 single with meals, $160 double without meals; Apr 20–Dec 19 $215 double with meals, $160 single with meals, $140 double without meals. DISC, MC, V. **Amenities:** Restaurant; bar service; bikes. *In room:* A/C, fridge.

4 MIDDLE CAICOS

The largest island in the TCI is also the least populated, and hotel/motel-type lodgings—not to mention restaurants, grocery stores, and shops—are almost nonexistent. Many visitors stay in rented villas. For a selection of villas, go to www.tcimall.tc/middlecaicos.

Tip: Don't forget to bring mosquito repellent, especially if you plan to visit some of the Middle Caicos Lucayan caves.

Blue Horizon Resort ★ Under new management, this little boutique resort with self-catering cottages enjoys one of the islands' most breathtaking locations, high on a green bluff overlooking the coral-sand swimming beach of Dragon Cay Cove and the blue-green waters of Mudjin Harbor. The resort comprises blue-tile-roofed cottages and villas dotting the hillside. The accommodations are modest, but the views from the cottage windows and patios are superb. Each of the two villas has two bedrooms and two bathrooms. Each of the five studio cottages has a kitchen, and Blue Horizon will arrange to have your groceries delivered to your cottage if you provide them with your grocery list 2 weeks before your arrival; you can buy fresh-caught fish and lobster from local fishermen once you arrive.

Middle Caicos Island, Turks and Caicos, B.W.I. ℂ **649/946-6141.** Fax 649/946-6139. www.bhresort.com. 7 units. $200–$325 daily; $1,400–$2,100 weekly. MC, V. **Amenities:** Concierge; grocery services; watersports equipment. *In room:* A/C (in some), TV, kitchen/kitchenettes, washer/dryer (in some).

Where to Dine in Providenciales & the Caicos Islands

You will eat very well in Provo—the quality and freshness of the food, much of it flown in daily, is remarkable for an island that has to import just about everything in the larder. But *you will pay to do so.* Yes, you can get a slice of pizza or a burger for a fairly reasonable price in a number of venues, but fast-food restaurants and chain eateries are virtually nonexistent here. It helps that many resorts and hotels offer fully equipped self-catering facilities, a way to offset the costs of paying for double-digit entree meals. Most resorts offer complimentary breakfasts as well, either full American style or Continental.

You can sample cuisines from around the world here, from Italian to Thai to Japanese. You will dine on dishes that have melded Continental-style cuisine with Caribbean influences. But if it's local flavor you're craving, head to Provo's Blue Hills (see "Dining Da Blue Hills," later in this chapter), where casual beach shacks serve such regional favorites as peas 'n' rice (or peas 'n' hominy); cod fish cakes; stewed fish; curry goat, fish, or chicken; johnnycakes (a sweet pan bread); all things conch (conch fritters, conch chowder, and conch ceviche); and all things lobster (in season). The food is fresh, good, and well-prepared, and you won't pay an arm and a leg for it. Or take a trip to the less-traveled islands of North Caicos and Middle Caicos, for solid local seafood (lobster, grouper, or cracked conch at Daniel's Café by the Sea in Middle) or traditional island meals prepared by celebrated home cooks (such as the Pelican Beach Hotel on North Caicos, where owner Susie Gardiner is happy to cook up your day's catch, accompanied by conch fritters and fruit cocktail cake). Try cooking up the local cuisine once you're back at home with a copy of the *Turks and Caicos Islands Food* cookbook (see "Turks & Caicos Islands Cookbook" sidebar, later in this chapter).

But what will you eat that actually *comes from* the Turks and Caicos? Like many other Caribbean nations, the TCI grows little of its own food except for personal use (on fertile North Caicos, locals grow corn, okra, and other crops and raise fruit trees). Most of what you eat in Provo restaurants is imported. Local hydroponic farms

WHERE TO DINE

4

PROVIDENCIALES

> ## ⓘ Tips Buying Spirits
>
> Liquor, liqueurs, wine, and beer are sold at liquor stores, gro-
> cery stores, and convenience stores (see "Shopping for Self-
> Catering" below for store locations and contact information),
> but no alcohol is sold in these venues on Sunday. Liquor by
> the drink, wine, and beer are available 7 days a week in res-
> taurants and bars. While you're on the islands, be sure to try
> the local beer, **Turk's Head,** produced in a microbrewery in
> Providenciales. It comes in a light, delicious lager and a heavier
> amber. *Note:* The legal drinking age is 18 on the islands.

provide restaurants with fresh lettuce, cucumbers, tomatoes, and
herbs. The true local bounty comes from the sea, in the form of fresh
conch, Caribbean lobster (in season, Aug–Mar), and a range of fish
from the local waters, such as red snapper, grouper, and mahimahi.

Keep in mind that the government adds an 11% tax on all restaurant bills. A few restaurants will add a service or gratuity charge,
particularly for tables of six or more people. Always check your bill
before tipping to make sure a gratuity has not already been figured in
to the total.

In general, Providenciales and the Caicos islands are not late-night
dining destinations. Most restaurants stop serving around 9pm to
10pm and close down altogether by 11pm.

1 PROVIDENCIALES

Most of the dining choices in Provo are found in the Grace Bay area.
Provo has two other good dining neighborhoods in Turtle Cove and
the Blue Hills; see listings below plus the "Dining Da Blue Hills" box
later in this chapter.

If you don't have a car and the restaurant is not within walking
distance, you can have your hotel call a taxi for you. For more information on getting around, see "Getting Around the Turks & Caicos
Islands," in chapter 2.

BLUE HILLS

Da Conch Shack ★ CONCH/CARIBBEAN   This happy spot is
set in and around a whitewashed beach shack on a sandy bluff above the
Blue Hills Beach. Next door is the open-air RumBar, separated by more
sand and white picnic tables. Down below, in the shallow aquamarine

waters, small conch pens hold live conch, refreshed daily by fishermen. On the beach the conch is drawn out of its shell and then served any number of ways, whether as superb conch fritters, conch curry, or conch chowder. Conch this fresh and well-prepared is a revelation. Equally good are the curry chicken, the lobster (in season), shrimp, or local grouper. Order up a platter of conch and an icy Turk's Head lager and then do as we say: Take off your shoes, press your face to the sun, and get mellow Da Conch Shack way.

Blue Hills. ✆ **649/946-8877.** www.conchshack.tc. No reservations. Conch, fish, chicken, and shrimp dishes $12–$14; lobster $28. No credit cards. Daily 11am–late.

Horse-Eye Jack's ★ CARIBBEAN This is another happening Blue Hills choice, with a great deck overlooking the Blue Hills Beach and the turquoise sea. (You can even check your e-mail with the free

Shopping for Self-Catering

Staying in Provo and have a full kitchen at your fingertips? Stock it with the following self-catering options. Located smack-dab in the center of Grace Bay is the fabulous new **Graceway Gourmet** (649/941-5000; www.gracewaygourmet. com), at the corner of Grace Bay Road and Dolphin Avenue, which sells all the basics—meats, vegetables, fruits, snacks, drinks—as well as a thoughtful selection of gourmet goods. Among its forward-thinking initiatives: North Caicos farmers sell fresh produce outside the store on the last Saturday of each month. The larger Graceway store, the **Graceway IGA** (✆ 649/941-5000; www.gracewayiga.com) is on Leeward Highway. (Keep in mind that these grocery stores are fully stocked with beer, wine, and liquor, but you can only buy alcohol in restaurants and bars on Sunday.) Buy fresh fish straight off the **Heaving Down Rocks Marina docks;** arrive at 5 or 6pm when the boats come in. Or head to **LTC Fisheries** (✆ 649/941-7358) in Five Cays. For liquor, beer, and wine, go to the **Wine & Spirits Liquor Store** (✆ 649/941-8047), in the Regent Village shopping plaza on Grace Bay Road; the **Tipsy Turtle,** in Turtle Cove Marina; or the **Wine Cellar** (✆ 649/946-4536), on Leeward Highway—you can also buy soft drinks and water at liquor stores. **Gourmet Catering** (✆ 649/941-4141; www.gourmetgoods.tc), in Grace Bay Court on Grace Bay Road, will prepare and serve complete catered dinners in your villa or condo.

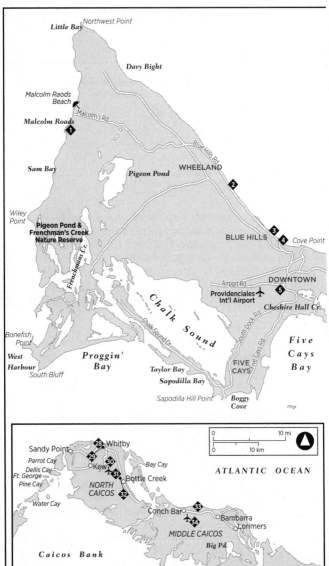

PROVIDENCIALES
Anacaona **19**
Atlantic Bar & Grill **10**
Baci Ristorante **7**
Bagatelle Bistrot **9**
Banana Boat Restaurant **7**
Bangkok Express **6**
Bay Bistro **15**
Beaches Turks & Caicos
  Resort restaurants **12**
Bella Luna **25**
Caicos Café **23**
Coco Bistro **27**
Coyaba Restaurant **22**
Da Conch Shack **3**
Fairways Bar & Grill **21**
Grace's Cottage **18**
Hemingway's on the Beach **16**
Hole in the Wall **5**
Horse-eye Jack's **4**
Jimmy's Dive Bar & Grill **24**
Magnolia Wine Bar & Restaurant **8**

Mango Reef **20**
Matsuri Sushi Bar **11**
O'Soleil **14**
Parallel23 **13**
Pizza Pizza **26**
The Restaurant at Amanyara **1**
Thai Orchid **17**
Three Queens **2**
The Vix Restaurant & Bar **17**

NORTH CAICOS
Miss B's Island Hut **32**
My Dee's **30**
Pelican Beach Hotel **28**
Silver Palm **29**
Super D's Café/Titters **31**

MIDDLE CAICOS
Daniel's Cafe **33**
Sapodilley's **34**

Wi-Fi while you're sipping a Turk's Head beer.) Sample the Jamaican-style jerk chicken, pork, or shrimp; seasoned and grilled kabobs; cracked shrimp (battered and fried); or one of the house burgers. Sunday is Family Day, with music, kite flying, beach volleyball, and more.

Blue Hills. ☎ 649/941-4955. No reservations. Conch dishes $9–$19. AE, MC, V. Daily 11am–late.

DOWNTOWN

Hole in the Wall ★ JAMAICAN/CARIBBEAN
This popular local hangout on Old Airport Road has some of the best island food on Provo. It's so good at preparing conch that it won the 2005 Conch Festival grand prize for the best overall conch dishes and best conch chowder—no mean feat in this conch-obsessed restaurant environment. You can get real island food here, from excellent jerk chicken or pork to fried fish, curry goat, and barbecued ribs. Sides include peas 'n' rice and fried plantains. Breakfast is the real island deal, with seasoned codfish, cornmeal porridge, peas 'n' grits, and johnnycakes. Hole in the Wall even offers free pickup/drop-off service to and from Grace Bay accommodations.

Downtown at Williams Plaza, Old Airport Rd. ☎ 649/941-4136. www.holeinthe wall-provo.com. No reservations. Main courses $12–$16. No credit cards. Mon–Sat 8am–late.

GRACE BAY

Newly opened in the Regent Village shopping plaza on Grace Bay Road is **The Vix Restaurant & Bar** (649/941-4144; daily lunch and dinner), with an intriguing modern menu (chicken tagine; slow-cooked pork belly; corn and crab risotto) and a carefully curated wine list. Its only drawback is a location in the middle of a shopping plaza—you can dine outside on an attractive landscaped patio but you still won't have beach or ocean views. If you love Thai food, the island's full-service Thai restaurant, **Thai Orchid** (☎ 649/946-4491; lunch and dinner Mon–Sat; dinner only Sun), also just opened in the Regent Village complex.

Very Expensive

Anacaona ★★★ EURO-CARIBBEAN Set beneath thatched-roof palapas and the starry evening sky, this is one of the top dining options in Provo. Among its winning attributes is an unbeatable location directly facing the Grace Bay Beach, which it shares with Grace Bay Club's two buzzing bars, the **Lounge** and the **Infinity Bar,** where you can enjoy a drink before dinner and watch the sun set. Tabletop candles and flickering lights from free-standing torches deepen the romance of the setting. The menu changes regularly, but you might start with the trio of conch (conch tacos, conch tempura, conch Creole)

Dining Out on an Evening Pass

Even if you're not staying there, you can sample the food at
Beaches Turks & Caicos Resort & Spa (p. 58) by purchasing
an evening pass. For $220 per adult ($140 per child), you can
enjoy all the food and drink you want from 6pm to 2:30am.
Just keep in mind that two of the restaurants, **Kimonos** (Japanese steakhouse) and **Sapodilla's** (the resort's signature
white-glove restaurant serving international cuisine), require
advance reservations (and book up quickly). Also keep in
mind that Sapodilla's is an adults-only eatery. Prefer to eat
breakfast and lunch and make a day of it at Beaches? Purchase a day pass for $200 adults ($130 per child), and from
9am to 5pm you can partake in the resort's numerous all-
inclusive watersports and other activities—a great option for
the kids in your party. For more information, call ℂ **649/946-
8000.**

or the tuna tartare; main courses rely heavily on seafood, particularly
fish—try the mahimahi en papillote or seared filet of red snapper. No
children 11 and under.

In the Grace Bay Club, 1 Grace Bay Circle Rd. ℂ **649/946-5050.** Reservations recommended. Main courses $28–$33. AE, MC, V. Daily 6:30–9pm.

Bagatelle ★★★ FRENCH MEDITERRANEAN FUSION
With nods to South Beach and downtown Manhattan, this urbane
spot takes TCI dining to a whole new level, with serious food and a
serious wine list served up in a monochromatic indoor/outdoor space
dotted with towering palm trees. The ambience is crisp and relaxed all
at once, with a sizzling up-tempo soundtrack that heats up as the day
progresses. But in the evening, when the sky is a canopy of stars and
shadows dance in the breeze, you are very much aware that you are in
Provo—and Provo at its most seductive. Start with the *crevettes à la
Thai* (grilled black tiger prawns), a cracked conch seared with a Viet-
namese red-pepper glaze, or the hearty West Indian vegetable curry.
Meats are impeccably prepared, like the roasted pork porterhouse or
the two-person *côte de boeuf.* The chef is a wizard with fish; he'll even
cook up your own catch of the day with a little advance notice. Only
a year old, this may be Provo's top destination restaurant.

In the Gansevoort Turks + Caicos, Lower Bight Rd. ℂ **649/946-5746.** www.
gansevoorttc.com. Reservations recommended. Main courses $31–$43. AE, MC, V.
Sun–Thurs 7am–10pm; Fri–Sat 7am–11pm.

Celebrating the Conch

The Caribbean Queen conch may be endangered elsewhere, but here in the Turks and Caicos, it's plentiful and a tasty staple for the creation of many dishes, whether served raw, fried, curried, or even jerked. Marvel at the versatility of conch and get a memorable taste of Blue Hills hospitality at the **Turks & Caicos Conch Festival,** held the last Saturday in November. Local restaurants vie to win top honors for best conch concoctions, including conch chowder, conch curry, and conch salad, to name a few of the contested dishes. In 2009 the Best in Festival honor was awarded to Bay Bistro (p. 93) and the Saltmills Diner took home the top spot for Best Conch Chowder (Hole in the Wall came in second). In its seventh year, the conch festival has become a popular celebration, with music, food, conch-blowing contests, and a heavenly Blue Hills beach location. For more information, go to **www.conchfestival.com**.

Coco Bistro ★★★ MEDITERRANEAN/CARIBBEAN This perennial favorite is so hot in the high season it recently turned away Bruce Willis and company (no reservation, alas). Coco Bistro is set in a former plant nursery that has since grown into the largest palm grove on the island. It's a magical spot: You dine outside under the palms, candles twinkling, and the food is as memorable as the ambience. Among the tasty starters, try conch, garlic, and potato soup scented with saffron; grilled shrimp satay on sugarcane skewers; or Peking duck egg rolls. For mains, try the roast rack of Colorado lamb with a pomegranate molasses and macadamia-nut crust; soft-shell-crab tempura; or a lively West Indian curry, brimming over with chicken and shrimp.

Grace Bay Rd. ✆ **649/946-5369.** www.cocobistro.tc. Reservations recommended. Main courses $28–$39. DISC, MC, V. Tues–Sun 6–10:30pm.

Coyaba Restaurant ★★ CONTINENTAL/CARIBBEAN When this popular gourmet restaurant moved from its longtime spot in Coral Gardens in October 2007, it barely missed a beat—it remains one of the island's most popular dining destinations. Its new location on the patio fronting the Caribbean Paradise Inn may not be as roomy as its previous locale, but that hasn't kept Chef Paul Newman (no, not that one) from flexing his inventive culinary chops. Chef Newman shows off his culinary flair in preparing some of the island's freshest and best seafood. His island dishes show a strong European influence. Start with coconut tempura shrimp in Barceló honey–rum sauce or the conch and seafood chowder. For a main course, the fish dishes are exuberantly flavored and exquisitely cooked; the Coyaba-style lobster thermidor is formidable.

Next to the Caribbean Paradise Inn, Grace Bay. ✆ **649/946-5186.** Reservations required. Main courses $32–$39. AE, MC, V. Wed–Mon 6–10pm.

Grace's Cottage ★★★ CARIBBEAN/CONTINENTAL   This buttery-yellow cottage with Victorian-style gingerbread trim and latticework is pure enchantment. The restaurant seats 62 people, but most every night, it's filled with hand-holding couples soaking up the palpable romantic ambience. Inside you can enjoy an aperitif at the mahogany bar before dinner. Dine on the cottage terrace or on one of the patios nestled in tropical vegetation amid softly illuminated lighting. After a sojourn serving a somewhat misguided menu of high-wire (and often goofy) culinary creations, Grace's Cottage has roared back with new executive chef Vincent Poitevin, whose food is flavorful and deeply satisfying. You might start with the Thai shellfish bisque or a nori tempura wrap of tuna and foie gras; mains include a slow-roasted South Caicos red snapper on a bed of jambalaya rice and the duxelles-encrusted rack of lamb on a wild-mushroom risotto.

In the Point Grace Hotel, Grace Bay. ✆ **649/946-5096.** Reservations required. Main courses $22–$45. AE, MC, V. Daily 6:30–10:30pm.

O'Soleil ★★★ INTERNATIONAL/ISLAND   When you hear good things about a restaurant from the local chefs, you know you're on to something. It's a showcase space, draped in white and accented with marble floors, crystal chandeliers, and vaulted ceilings—quite a departure from the island-style interiors of other local spots. The space is coolly elegant, but veers ever so slightly into Carmela Soprano territory—a little too much white and crystal and more white for us. We prefer to dine on the alfresco terraces; the patio out front faces the croquet lawn, and the one on the restaurant's backside is enveloped in greenery and has a soothing waterfall wall. The food is splendid, prepared with flair and confidence by one of the island's few female chefs, Lauren Callighen. Start with the tequila-cured salmon or the pistachio-crusted, pan-fried scallops. Entrees include a curried grouper in a lime curry sauce; a Caribbean shrimp tagliatelle; and terrific New York steak, here in a wild-mushroom demi-glace. The service is superb.

In the Somerset on Grace Bay resort, Grace Bay. ✆ **649/946-5900.** Reservations recommended. Main courses $28–$40. AE, DC, MC, V. Daily 7:30–10:30am and 6–10pm.

Parallel23 ★★★ TROPICAL FUSION/INTERNATIONAL   We love the summer-garden-party ambience of this place. Try to snag a table on the restaurant terrace, entwined in flower vines and lit by gas lamps specially ordered from a shop in New Orleans. It's a bewitching setting, overlooking the glittering Palm Place courtyard and situated in the Mansion, the Regent Palms resort's stately homage to Caribbean Great Houses of old. The menu neatly balances top-end foods (impeccably sourced aged steaks and Wisconsin veal) with creative, reasonably priced nightly specials. It's a thoughtful menu: the butter alone is whipped with Parmesan and truffle oil. Starters include yellowfin tuna sashimi or pan-seared foie gras. On the grill menu, you choose your grilled meat and then sides and toppings. The attached **Green Flamingo Bar** (open noon–midnight) has the kind of over-stuffed sofas and dark-grain wood you'd find in a gentlemen's club in some exotic colonial outpost.

In the Regent Palms resort, Grace Bay. ℂ **649/946-8666.** Reservations required. Main courses $18–$38. AE, MC, V. Daily 7–10:30am and 6–10:30pm.

Expensive

Caicos Café ★★ CARIBBEAN/FRENCH   This is a favorite spot among locals, but visitors also find the warm, romantic ambience and good food hard to resist. It's set on the terrace deck of what appears to be a Caribbean cottage with gingerbread trim, gaily illuminated with strings of twinkling lights and flaming torches. Colorful Haitian artwork blankets the walls. The menu reflects the French/Mediterranean influences of its chef/owner Pierrik Marziou. But the vibe is pure Turks and Caicos, a leisurely and low-key approach to dining and life in general. Fresh seafood is a big draw; the conch chowder is a big, hearty meal in itself. Also good are the conch Creole, shrimp Caicos (spicy jumbo shrimp served with a seafood risotto and veggies), and seafood gumbo (shrimp, lobster, scallops, fish, mussels, with tomato and vegetables).

Caicos Café Plaza, Grace Bay Rd. ℂ **649/946-5278.** Reservations recommended. Main courses $26–$36. MC, V. Tues–Sat noon–3pm; Mon–Sat 5–11pm. Closed Sept–Oct and 2 weeks in June.

Moderate

Atlantic Bar & Grill ★ Finds CARIBBEAN   This modest and unpretentious outdoor bar and grill has only nine tables and is really designed as an amenity for West Bay Club guests—but we think it's a little gem. The restaurant has practically no room for food storage, so everything is delivered fresh daily. The chefs (one of whom cooked for Dubai royalty) prepare tasty and fresh island specialties, not to mention a creamy shrimp linguine and a nice fat rib-eye steak; daily specials depend on what rolls into the pantry that morning. An outdoor grill is employed to cook up pizzas, cheesecakes, pies, even cookies. The bar is small but very convivial.

In the West Bay Club resort, Lower Bight, Grace Bay. ✆ **649/946-8550.** Main
courses $24–$35. AE, MC, V. Daily 7–10:30am, 11:30am–3:30pm, and 6–9pm.

Bay Bistro ★ CARIBBEAN/EUROPEAN   The location here is
fantastic, directly overlooking Grace Bay Beach. You'll practically be
kissed by sea spray as you dine. In fact, you can enter from the beach,
along a wooden plank. It's a lovely, casual spot, set in a whitewashed
wooden open-air porch above Grace Bay beach. Food is hearty and
good, featuring an assortment of standard Caribbean specialties
(conch fingers, fish wrap, snapper, tuna, and mahimahi), steak,
chicken, and rack of lamb. Tasty starters include divine conch wont-
ons and the Princess conch and mushroom crepes. The Bay Bistro
serves food practically all day long, from hearty breakfasts to lunch
and dinner; have a drink at **Junior's Bar** before dinner. One slightly
jarring note: Service can be spotty.

In the Sibonné hotel, on Grace Bay. ✆ **649/946-5396.** Reservations recommended. Main courses $25–$34. AE, MC, V. Daily 7am–10pm.

Bella Luna ★ ITALIAN   Situated up in "the glass house" on a
slight rise along Grace Bay Road, Bella Luna provides yet another of
Provo's many atmospheric dining experiences. Chef Cosimo Tipodi
gives his Italian menu a few subtle Caribbean tweaks. You can start
with beef carpaccio or conch *frittelle,* grilled conch patties with a jerk
mayo sauce. Veal and chicken are served a number of classic Italian
ways. Pastas are recommended, particularly seafood pastas like the
linguine *tuttomare,* with fresh lobster (in season only) and shrimp
with your choice of sauce: marinara, cream, or rosé. Linguine *mare-
chiaro* is basically linguine in clam sauce with a kicky spiciness. Week-
day lunch is served here in high season only.

Grace Bay Rd., Grace Bay. ✆ **649/946-5214.** Reservations recommended. Main
courses $22–$30. AE, MC, V. Mon–Sat 6–10pm.

Fairways Bar & Grill (Finds CARIBBEAN/CONTINENTAL
With all the ocean-side/oceanfront/oceanview dining available in
Provo, why on earth would you want to dine on a golf course? Well,
if you could find one this congenial, you needn't ask. In fact, you can
eat here all day if you really want—the restaurant is open from 7am
to 10pm, and in between the bar serves hearty snacks. The bright,
airy, high-ceilinged space has French doors that open onto an outdoor
patio with seating overlooking the golf course greens. The menu is
extensive; choose from chicken curry, baby-back ribs, and a seafood
linguine; Friday-night Pub Nights feature bangers and mash, shep-
herd's pie, and fish and chips.

Provo Golf & Country Club, Grace Bay Rd. ✆ **649/946-5833.** Reservations
requested. Main courses $16–$28. AE, MC, V. Daily 7am–9pm.

Dining Da Blue Hills

The welcoming beach-shack bar/restaurants along the Reef Harbor shoreline of northwest Provo represent what one local describes as a "taste of old-time Provo." For a thera-peutic immersion in the TCI art of studied languor, you can't beat a meal at one of the shacks in Provo's oldest settlement along the rural Blue Hills road, dotted with pastel-painted churches and schools. In fact, many visitors come here straight from the airport, kicking off their cold-weather armor and city-slicker shoes to dig their toes in the warm sand, stare out at the sun-dappled azure seas, and dine on conch freshly pulled from the sea. Even better, the food at these shacks is as fresh and soul-satisfying as anything you'll find in Provo. **Horse-Eye Jack's** has a deck overlooking the beach and Jamaican-style jerk meat (see review, earlier in this chapter), and **Da Conch Shack** is where live conch is held in pens in the shallows below and brought up to order (see review, earlier in this chapter). The oldest of the Blue Hills restaurants, **Three Queens,** is a favorite local hangout, especially on Friday nights. Hours for all the Blue Hills shacks vary, so call before you go, but the general opening times are Monday to Saturday from 11am until past sunset. Bring cash.

Hemingway's on the Beach ★ CARIBBEAN/INTERNATIONAL
This place has been so consistent for so long that it's disheartening to get reports of unhappy diners. Yes, for a certain discriminating diner, Hemingway's comes up short. This casual open-air place is jumping morning to night, and the ocean-side location is a big enticement; it would be a real shame if the food and service are no longer up to the setting. The coconut shrimp is still light and tasty, and if local lobster is in season, order it here, grilled. Hemingway's is also a fine lunch choice, serving a terrific mango shrimp salad over Provo lettuce with mango chutney, a very respectable hamburger, and satisfying chicken and chips: marinated and fried Caribbean jerk chicken breast with the restaurant's signature seasoned fries. At night, torches and candlelight heighten the ambience. A bell mounted on a pole on the upper deck of the restaurant is there to ring if anyone spots JoJo the resident dolphin cruising Grace Bay.

Mango Reef ★ (**Kids**) CARIBBEAN/INTERNATIONAL   This
pleasant, laid-back spot is not luxe by any means and has no ocean
views (it overlooks the pool and lush gardens at the Royal West Indies
Resort). But if you come for lunch or dinner, you may find yourself
surrounded by TCI movers and shakers chowing down heartily on a
Mango Reef meal. That's because the food is reliably delicious and
won't drain your bank account dry. It's a big menu, with lots of seafood, including conch (fritters, chowder, salad, and cracked) and a
Red Queen snapper curry. Caribbean pork comes with fresh pineap-
ple salsa. At lunch you can also choose among panini, wraps, fajitas,
burgers, and sandwiches. A kids-friendly spot, too.

Royal West Indies Resort, Grace Bay Rd. ✆ **649/946-8200.** www.mangoreef.com.
Reservations recommended. Main courses $21–$32. AE, MC, V. Daily 8am–10pm.

Matsuri Sushi Bar ★ SUSHI/JAPANESE   Sushi lovers swear by
the sushi served at this island outpost, next to the Graceway IGA. You
can get set dinners of sushi, sashimi, rolls, or combos. A number of
rolls are available, from standard California to spicy octopus. This
may be one of the few places in the sushi world where you can get a
conch maki. The owners have also opened a restaurant in the Saltmills
on Grace Bay Road, **Yoshi's Japanese Restaurant,** with a similar
menu and hours (✆ **649/941-3374**).

101 Graceway House (next to the Graceway IGA), Leeward Hwy. ✆ **649/941-
3274.** Main courses $14–$39; sushi rolls $6–$16. DISC, MC, V. Mon–Sat noon–3pm
and 6–10pm.

Inexpensive
Bangkok Express THAI   The food is surprisingly good at this
inexpensive Thai restaurant in Provo, opened by a Bangkok expat. Try
such specialties as massaman curry shrimp, satay chicken, basil seafood, and Siam rolls.

Provo Plaza, Leeward Hwy. ✆ **649/946-4491.** Main courses $17–$20. AE, DISC,
MC, V. Daily 11am–3pm and 5–10pm.

Jimmy's Dive Bar & Grill AMERICAN   Jimmy, a New Yorker
who got fed up with 21st-century life in the Big Apple, runs this lively
little bar and grill. It opens early and stays open later than most to feed
the folks who arrive in Provo on the last flights of the day. Jimmy wanted
to create a Provo version of a diner and, in keeping with the diner ethos,
serves breakfast, lunch, and dinner. This is probably the only place on the
island where you can get both a Philly cheese sub *and* cracked conch.

Ports of Call shopping plaza, Grace Bay Rd. ✆ **649/946-52822.** Sandwiches $11–
$17; main courses $12–$45. MC, V. Sun–Wed 7am–11pm; Thurs–Sat 7am–midnight.

Island Scoop: Locally Made Ice Cream

For a sugary frozen treat and a break from the island heat, try one of the locally made ice creams and sorbets at **Island Scoop**. Fill a cone with traditional flavors such as chocolate or peach or try something a little more exotic like white mint. You can also get a range of shakes, smoothies, sundaes, and cookies. You'll find two Provo locations: Grace Bay Plaza (*© 649/242-8511*) and in Downtown Providenciales, next to Hole in the Wall restaurant (*© 649/243-5051*).

Pizza Pizza   Craving pizza after a week of conch? Pizza Pizza brings it all back home to you with solid hot brick-oven pies and your favorite toppings—plus a few interesting less-familiar choices, like the Seafood Pizza, weighted down with squid, conch, mussels, clams, shrimp, crab, baby octopus, and garlic. The pizza dough is made fresh daily, and the menu includes a full complement of Italian entrees: pastas, lasagna, baked ziti, and grilled panini. It's right on Grace Bay Road, which makes a convenient spot for pickup (or delivery) to your Grace Bay hotel; you can also dine in on the gaily lighted second-floor terrace. It has another location at Cinema Plaza on Leeward Highway (*© 649/941-3577*).

Grace Bay Plaza. *© 649/941-8010.* Medium pizzas $15–$18, large pizzas $17–$26. Daily 11:30am–late.

NORTHWEST POINT

The **Restaurant at Amanyara** ★★ accepts non-resort guests, but you must reserve at least 2 days in advance. The menu features Asian- and Mediterranean-infused cuisine (with an emphasis on local sea-food) and is served either indoors or on a terrace overlooking the water at Northwest Point. Arrive early so that you can have a drink on the bar terrace and watch the sunset. Call *© 649/941-8133* to reserve a table.

TURTLE COVE

Note: At press time, the much-admired **Aqua Bar & Terrace** had closed, replaced by the Anchorage Bar & Grill (*© 649/241-9140*). Aqua owner/chef Clive Whent is now a full-time presence at his other restaurant, Bay Bistro (see above).

Baci Ristorante ★ ITALIAN   This spot enjoys one of the pretti-est waterside settings in Provo, on the docks of the Turtle Cove

Marina. Lacy iron doors lead out to terraced outdoor seating overlooking the water. The tasty cuisine, the romantic patio, the stone floors and wrought-iron entrance, and the whirling *Casablanca*-style overhead fans conspire to make this an agreeable stopover. Veal is served four different ways: in lemon butter sauce, in a red-wine peppercorn sauce, in a Marsala-and-mushroom sauce, or baked and topped with tomato sauce and mozzarella. The hearty pasta dishes include the usual suspects: fettuccine Alfredo, for example, and penne a la vodka (here with chicken). Baci also has kid-friendly brick-oven pizza, with plenty of toppings to choose from.

Turtle Cove Marina, Harbour Towne. ✆ **649/941-3044.** Reservations recommended. Lunch $10–$18; main courses $19–$27 (lobster in season commands market prices). AE, MC, V. Mon–Fri noon–2:30pm and Mon–Sat 6–10pm; closed Sun.

Banana Boat Restaurant CARIBBEAN/SEAFOOD The Banana Boat is not the best restaurant on the island, but it's certainly one of the most convivial—there's not a yachtie on Provo who hasn't moored here to enjoy an island meal and a potent tropical drink. For a main course, you might try T-bone steak, cracked conch, or some freshly caught local fish. At lunch, favorites include lobster salad or a half-pound burger. No one in the kitchen fusses too much with these dishes, and here that's a good thing: Expect fresh and flavorful food. A choice seat is on the timber-and-plank veranda that juts out over piers on Turtle Cove. On Tuesdays, prices for all entrees are cut in half, and Saturday is karaoke night.

Turtle Cove Marina. ✆ **649/941-5706.** Lunch $6.50–$15; main courses $12–$26. AE, MC, V. Daily 11am–11pm.

Magnolia Restaurant & Wine Bar ★★ MEDITERRANEAN/ASIAN/INTERNATIONAL You won't find a setting like this anywhere else on the flat scrublands of Provo: high on a hill overlooking Turtle Cove Marina, with the sparkling lights of the island spread out before you. You could almost be dining in a cliff-side trattoria overlooking the Mediterranean Sea. Magnolia has established itself as one of the best places to dine in Provo—and new chef Matt Gaynor is continuing the tradition of excellence. Try the sesame-seed-and-cracked-pepper-crusted rare seared tuna or the bacon-wrapped, pesto-stuffed pork tenderloin. Start with a bracing version of Turks and Caicos–style seafood chowder, tempura shrimp, or a stack of grilled vegetables and mozzarella.

At the Miramar Resort, Turtle Cove Marina. ✆ **649/941-5108.** Reservations recommended. Main courses $24–$34. AE, MC, V. Tues–Sun 6–10pm. Wine bar opens at 5pm.

Turks & Caicos Islands Cookbook

If you want to take home treasured recipes from the Turks and Caicos Islands, from both professional and celebrated local home cooks, look for a copy of the **Turks and Caicos Islands Food** cookbook, a colorful hardcover published in 2005 by the Turks & Caicos Islands Red Cross ($20; proceeds go to support the Red Cross). Among the recipes are Love's Fried Fish with Tamarind Sauce, from Isadora Emanuel (known as Love), who runs Love's Restaurant in South Caicos; island jerk encrusted Chilean sea bass, from executive chef Alberto Artiles at Grace's Cottage in the Point Grace resort; and Pat's Dreamy Coleslaw, from Pat Simmons of Pat's Place in Salt Cay. You can buy the cookbook through the Red Cross or at various resorts throughout the islands and in the Unicorn Bookstore on Leeward Highway in Provo.

2 NORTH & MIDDLE CAICOS

Currently, the restaurant choices in North or Middle Caicos are slim but choice; these are great places to sample island cuisine.

NORTH CAICOS

In Whitby, **Pelican Beach Hotel** (© 649/946-7112) serves home-made meals prepared by the owner, Susie Gardiner; you must call ahead to reserve a table. The **Silver Palm** restaurant (© 649/946-7113; www.oceanbeach.tc), also in Whitby, is a full-service restaurant with a menu that includes conch dishes (chowder, fritters, cracked conch), grilled or pan-fried fish, lobster (in season), and homemade breads and desserts.

Two recommended local spots to catch a bite to eat are both near the airport: **My Dee's Restaurant & Bar** (Airport Rd.; © 649/946-7059), which serves local food like conch, fish, lobster, and peas 'n' rice and is open daily for breakfast, lunch, and dinner; you'll need reservations for Sunday brunch and dinner; and **Miss B's Island Hut** (Airport Rd.; © 649/946-7727), which serves native island cuisine and is open daily for breakfast, lunch, and dinner. **Super D Café** (© 649/946-7258), the restaurant in the airport, offers local food.

Middle Caicos has largely self-catering options, although **Sapodilley's,** a small restaurant at the Middle Caicos airport, offers a few local specialties and a bar.

Daniel's Café by the Sea   This local spot has a lovely patio with sea views and delicious local seafood (cracked conch is one recommended dish), homemade bread, and a laidback Middle Caicos vibe. The proprietor is Daniel O. Forbes, who also owns the Middle Caicos Co-op.

Conch Bar Village, Middle Caicos. ℂ **649/946-6132**. Reservations recommended for dinner. Main courses $10-$20. Tues–Sun 11:30am–2:30pm (call for dinner reservations on Fri and Sat).

5

Exploring Providenciales & the Caicos Islands

Most of the country's celebrated sports and activities revolve around, unsurprisingly, its ubiquitous resource: all that crystal-clear water with the mesmerizing emerald hue. Try scuba diving the spectacular underwater walls just offshore, fishing the coral reef or deepwater drop-offs, or leisurely exploring the little uninhabited cays and coves that dot the watery landscape.

Of course, there are plenty of nonwatersports-related things to do here, including golf, tennis, horseback riding, exploring historical attractions, caving, shopping, and enjoying state-of-the-art spa treatments. This chapter tells you how to explore the best the islands have to offer.

1 BEACHES

It's no hype: The beaches of the Turks and Caicos are some of the most beautiful on the planet, thanks in large part to one of the few remaining unspoiled coral reef ecosystems in the Caribbean—or the world for that matter. This, the third-largest coral reef system on the planet, helps act as a breakwater against ocean surges for these islands, keeping the coastal waters calm and clear. It makes its presence known on land as well: Coral is literally the soft white sand beneath your feet.

The Caicos islands have some of the country's best beaches, including world-class Grace Bay—and on many of them, yours will be the only footprints you'll see.

Note: All Turks and Caicos Island beaches are public, and even the most developed residential beaches are required to have public access points. These access routes are for public use; never cross private property to get to a beach.

PROVIDENCIALES

Starting at Leeward and running all the way to Thompson Cove, **Grace Bay Beach** ★★★ is Provo's finest beach and, some say, one of the finest beaches on the planet. Alongside 19km (12 miles) of spectacular, powdery-soft white sand are gin-clear, blue-green seas that are extremely tranquil and free of rocks, making the beach ideal for young kids. Many resorts have developed along its edge, so you won't have these sands all to yourself. Though there are no public facilities on the beach, the hotels themselves come in handy, because all have restrooms and bars serving tropical drinks.

Smith's Reef, near the Turtle Cove Marina, and Bight Reef, directly in front of the Coral Gardens resort, are two excellent snorkeling spots right on Grace Bay.

Grace Bay Beach is so stunning that you might not want to venture anywhere else, but a few other beaches on the island are worth a look. In the east, **Long Bay Beach** lies on the opposite shore from Grace Bay, opening onto Long Bay itself. It begins around Juba Point and extends east to Stubbs Cove and is virtually free of hotels (but is a growing residential area). The shallow waters here are very sheltered and have virtually no waves, making it perfect for young children. Take a horse-back ride on the beach here with Provo Ponies (see nearby box).

If you really crave privacy, seek out **Malcolm Beach.** The traditional way to see this charming cove (often referred to as Malcolm Roads Beach) is by 4×4 along twisting, bumpy Malcolm Roads. You can also access the beach by staying at Amanyara (the resort is adjacent to the beach) or by getting a tour-boat operator to take you there. Its waters are part of the Northwest Point Marine National Park. There's good snorkeling, though you'll have to bring your own gear—unless, of course, you're a guest at Amanyara, which has excellent snorkeling and other watersports equipment. Be sure to lock valuables in the trunk of the car before you head to the beach.

Chalk Sound, a landlocked lagoon west of Five Cays Settlement, has been turned into a public park. The hamlet of Five Cays itself boasts a small harbor and a modern airport. **Sapodilla Bay** and **Taylor Bay** are part of Chalk Sound National Park. These beautiful, shallow bays along Provo's southwest coastline have soft, silty bottoms and warm water. Sapodilla Bay lies between two 9m (30-ft.) cliffs at Gussy Cove, stretching all the way west to Ocean Point. This is such a well-protected beach—with fine sands and clear shallow water (even 30m/98 ft. out)—that the locals often refer to it as "the children's beach."

CAICOS CAYS

Pine Cay's perfect crescent of pale white sand is a marketer's dream. This private island is home to the **Meridian Club** (p. 79) and a number of private homes. **Parrot Cay** is another gorgeous private island, this one with an eponymous resort with a celebrity clientele and fabulous spa.

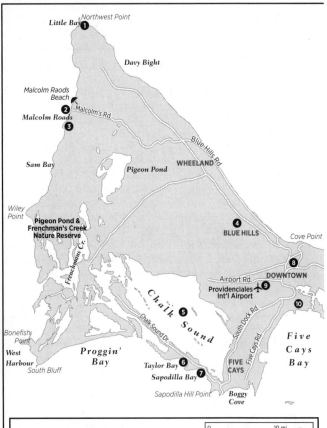

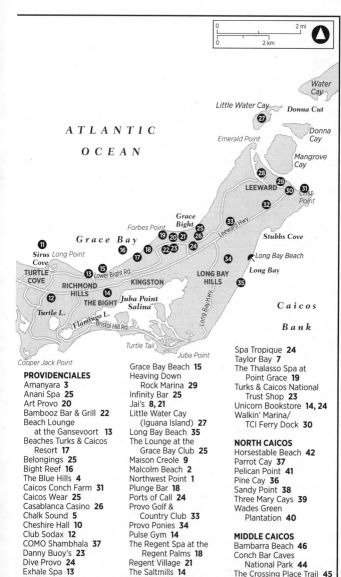

PROVIDENCIALES
Amanyara **3**
Anani Spa **25**
Art Provo **20**
Bambooz Bar & Grill **22**
Beach Lounge
    at the Gansevoort **13**
Beaches Turks & Caicos
    Resort **17**
Belongings **25**
Bight Reef **16**
The Blue Hills **4**
Caicos Conch Farm **31**
Caicos Wear **25**
Casablanca Casino **26**
Chalk Sound **5**
Cheshire Hall **10**
Club Sodax **12**
COMO Shambhala **37**
Danny Buoy's **23**
Dive Provo **24**
Exhale Spa **13**
FunWorld **32**
Gilley's **9, 28**

Grace Bay Beach **15**
Heaving Down
    Rock Marina **29**
Infinity Bar **25**
Jai's **8, 21**
Little Water Cay
    (Iguana Island) **27**
Long Bay Beach **35**
The Lounge at the
    Grace Bay Club **25**
Maison Creole **9**
Malcolm Beach **2**
Northwest Point **1**
Plunge Bar **18**
Ports of Call **24**
Provo Golf &
    Country Club **33**
Provo Ponies **34**
Pulse Gym **14**
The Regent Spa at the
    Regent Palms **18**
Regent Village **21**
The Saltmills **14**
Sapodilla Bay **36**
Smith's Reef **11**

Spa Tropique **24**
Taylor Bay **7**
The Thalasso Spa at
    Point Grace **19**
Turks & Caicos National
    Trust Shop **23**
Unicorn Bookstore **14, 24**
Walkin' Marina/
    TCI Ferry Dock **30**

NORTH CAICOS
Horsestable Beach **42**
Parrot Cay **37**
Pelican Point **41**
Pine Cay **36**
Sandy Point **38**
Three Mary Cays **39**
Wades Green
    Plantation **40**

MIDDLE CAICOS
Bambarra Beach **46**
Conch Bar Caves
    National Park **44**
The Crossing Place Trail **45**
Middle Caicos Co-op **45**
Mudjin Harbor **43**

Horseback Riding on the Beach

The newly paved Long Bay Highway leads up into the Long Bay Hills, home of **Provo Ponies,** which offers **horseback rides on the beach** ★★ for novices and seasoned riders alike. The Provo Ponies stables comprise a real menagerie, with friendly dogs roaming, roosters crowing, and 18 horses—technically big ponies—available to ride.

On our afternoon ride, we were assigned horses according to skill levels. I'm a less-experienced rider, so I was given a handsome but slightly lumbering animal. Let's just say this old gentleman's days as a Triple Crown threat are behind him. But even my gallant steed picked up the pace when we hit the beach; the horses love the gentle sand, the cool breezes, and the open spaces. As do the riders: It's a relaxing, soul-satisfying experience.

Camille Slattery, the energetic owner of Provo Ponies, came to the Turks and Caicos 19 years ago to teach scuba diving and never left. Her stable grew along with her love of horses; she opened to the public in 2002. Many of her horses are Grand Turk horses, which Camille calls "bomb-proof: so easy and so intelligent." A couple she even refers to as "babysitters"—they literally take care of the people riding them. These horses can take the heat because they're born and bred here; still, the stable doesn't schedule any midday rides, for the benefit of both horse and rider. Provo Ponies offers two rides a day along the secluded, untrammeled Long Bay beach, in morning and late afternoon. Rides last an hour or 80 minutes, and helmets, fanny packs, and water are provided. They take beginners or experts—and only allow cantering if the rider shows he or she is experienced. They also offer private swimming rides. What is it about riding a horse on a tropical beach? As Camille says, "It's everybody's fantasy." For more information, call ✆ **649/241-6350** or 649/946-5252 or go to www.provo ponies.com (Long Bay Hills, off Dolphin Lane; 1-hr. ride $75; 90-min. ride $90; hotel pickup/drop-off included; rides Mon–Sat 9:30am and 4:30pm; 11 riders maximum per trip; maximum 200-lb. weight limit; children 5 and under must have previous riding experience).

You may touch down on one of the lovely uninhabited cays of the Caicos Cays with one of the many half- or full-day beach excursions offered by a number of watersports operators in the area. Many of these cays are part of TCI national parkland, and all have beautiful, fine-powder beaches. Among them: **Little Water Cay,** a nature reserve that is home to a population of native rock iguanas (see "A Visit to Iguana Island," later in this chapter), and **Fort George Cay,** a National Historic Site. The high-rent development of **Dellis Cay** as a Mandarin Oriental hotel and upscale private homes was on hold at press time.

NORTH CAICOS

Up until now, only those in the know found their way to **Sandy Point,** a crescent of perfect beach within sight of the Parrot Cay resort. At press time, it was unclear whether construction on the resort and condo complex Royal Reef Resort would continue.

Just east of Sandy Point, the coves of **Three Mary Cays** (named for its three distinctive rocks) are prime snorkeling spots. In Whitby, step into the shallows of the palm-fringed **Pelican Point beach** (in front of Pelican Beach Hotel) and find conch shells of every size. Also in Whitby, lovely **Horsestable Beach** enjoyed its North Caicos seclusion for years (it's also a prime bird-watching spot).

MIDDLE CAICOS

The soft green cliffs overlooking the sea in **Mudjin Harbor** provide a dramatic departure from the dry, flat scrublands of Provo. Down below, Dragon Cay has coves set amid turquoise shallows that make for perfect snorkeling and swimming. Travel along the old Conch Bar on bluffs above the shoreline until you reach **Bambarra Beach,** where casuarina pines fringe a white-sand beach; at low tide a long sandbar stretches from the beach to Pelican Cay.

2 SCUBA DIVING & SNORKELING

SCUBA DIVING ★★★

Dive experts, including the late Jacques Cousteau, have cited Providenciales as one of the 10 best sites in the world. Why is the diving so good in Provo and the Turks and Caicos in general? A number of reasons: great visibility (often more than 30m/100 ft.), gentle seas, a barrier reef that runs the full length of the island's 27km (17-mile) north coast, dramatic vertical underwater "walls" where the coral is big and healthy and marine life congregates, and a local government committed to protecting its natural assets—much of the coastal

Caicos Watersports Operators: Master List

Watersports activities are the name of the game in the Turks and Caicos, and in most cases you'll be availing yourself of the capable expertise of local watersports operators and boat charters to get out and play in the miles of sea, whether you're on a scuba-diving or snorkeling expedition, parasailing or sailing, enjoying an eco-adventure, visiting other islands, or simply taking one of the extremely popular beach cruises and excursions that combine any number of activities. Much of the coral reef is protected national parkland and the water too shallow in spots to allow powerboats and personal watercraft to be rented out without a captain aboard—with a few exceptions in designated spots. **Sun & Fun Sea Sports** (© **649/946-5724;** www.turks andcaicos.tc/sunandfun) rents out motorboats and personal watercraft for use in designated areas.

Many of the "beach excursion" boat trips are half-day or day-long cruises that offer a variety of activities, from snorkeling and shelling to beach barbecues, conch diving, and visits to Little Water Cay, or "Iguana Island," as it's also known, a nature reserve where a population of endangered native rock iguanas enjoys protected status (see "A Visit to Iguana Island," later in this chapter).

The following is a master list of the top watersports and charter-boat operators in Providenciales and the Caicos islands, their contact information, and a general description of the types of services they have to offer. Most include free pickup/drop-off from your hotel to the marina and back in the price of the excursions.

- **After Five Concierge** (© **800/833-1341** in the U.S. or 649/232-3483; www.after5.tc): Private dive instruction; personalized watersports tours; sunset cruises; beach excursions; fishing charters; eco-tours.
- **Art Pickering's Provo Turtle Divers** (© **800/833-1341** in the U.S. or 649/946-4232; www.provoturtledivers.com): Scuba diving, instruction, and equipment rental; snorkeling.
- *Beluga* **Charter Sailing** (© **649/946-4396;** www.sail beluga.com): Captained charter sailing on a Polynesian catamaran; beach excursions.
- **Big Blue Unlimited** (© **649/946-5034;** www.bigblue unlimited.com or www.bigblue.tc): Technical and recreational scuba diving, instruction, and equipment rental;

eco-adventures (including kayaking, snorkeling, mountain biking, and North Caicos trips); private charters.

- **Blue Whale Tours & Excursions** (© **649/331-5027;** http:// bluewhaleexcursions.com): West Caicos snorkeling; beach excursions; bonefishing and deep-sea fishing; glowworm tours.
- **Caicos Adventures** (Regent Village; © **649/941-3346;** www.tcidiving.com): Scuba diving, instruction, and equipment rental; snorkeling; and beach excursions.
- **Catch the Wave** (© **649/941-3047;** www.catchthe wavecharters.mobi): Bonefishing and bottom fishing; beach excursions; water-skiing; island safaris (including cave and bird-watching trips); private charters.
- **Dive Provo** (© **800/234-7768** in the U.S. or 649/946-5040; www.diveprovo.com): Technical and recreational scuba diving, instruction, and equipment rental; hotel/ dive packages; snorkeling.
- **Kenard Cruises** (© **649/232-3866;** www.KenardCruises. com): Customized luxury cruises with Captain Kenard in a power catamaran.
- **KiteProvo** (© **649/242-2927;** www.kiteprovo.com) offers kiteboarding lessons with certified instructors as well as rentals.
- **Ocean Vibes** (© **649/231-6636** or 649/331-1104; www. oceanvibes.com): Scuba diving, instruction, and equipment rental; scuba and snorkeling charters; multiday packages.
- **Reef Peepers** (© **649/2311-4961;** www.reefpeepers. com): Glass-bottom-boat excursions; snorkeling trips; sunset wine-and-cheese cruises; private charters.
- **Sail Provo** (© **649/946-4783;** www.sailprovo.com): Sailing cruises; snorkeling cruises; combination beach excursion cruises; glowworm cruises; sunset cruises; weddings.
- **Silver Deep** (© **649/946-5612;** www.silverdeep.com): Scuba diving; snorkeling; bonefishing, bottom fishing, fly-fishing, deep-sea fishing, night fishing, and shark fishing; beach excursions and barbecues; glowworm cruises; sunset cruises; island getaways; private charters.
- **Sun Charters** (© **649/231-0624;** www.suncharters.tc): Sailing cruises and beach excursions aboard the *Atabeyra;* pirate cruises; private charters; weddings.
- **Windsurfing Provo** (in front of the Ocean Club East resort; © **649/241-1687;** www.windsurfingprovo.tc) offers kiteboarding and windsurfing lessons and rentals.

Tips **Websites for Divers**

For useful information on scuba diving in the Caribbean, check out the website of the **Professional Association of Diving Instructors (PADI)** at **www.padi.com**. This site provides descriptions of dive destinations throughout the Caribbean and a directory of PADI-certified dive operators. *Scuba Diving Magazine* also has a helpful website at **www.scuba diving.com**. Both sites list dive-package specials and display gorgeous color photos of some of the most beautiful dive spots in the world.

waters around Provo are protected national parkland, where fishing is not allowed. The water is warm and calm much of the year.

From the shore at Grace Bay, visitors can see where the sea breaks along 23km (14 miles) of barrier reef, the teeming undersea home to sea life that ranges from swarms of colorful schools of fish to barracuda to rotund grouper.

Around Provo and the Caicos islands, the popular diving spots include **Grace Bay, Northwest Point** (a 4.8km/3-mile strip of excellent dive sites with a vertical drop-off to 2,099m/6,888 ft.), **Pine Cay, West Caicos** (with miles of 1,829m/6,000-ft. vertical walls), and **French Cay** (more 6,000-ft. vertical drop-offs). The latter two are great spots to see large pelagics such as reef sharks, sea turtles, stingrays, and dolphins. For extensive information about each of these sites, go to the very informative website of **Art Pickering's Provo Turtle Divers Ltd.,** Turtle Cove (© **649/946-4232** or 800/833-1341 for reservations; www.provoturtledivers.com). It's the oldest dive operation in the islands.

Most dive operators rent scuba tanks, plus backpacks and weight belts (included in the dive cost). In general, a single-tank dive costs $75, a night dive goes for $85, and a morning two-tank dive is $109-$119. Many offer technical diving and PADI training, with full instruction and resort courses. An open-water PADI referral course goes for $400.

SNORKELING ★★★

The snorkeling is as good as it is on Provo and the Caicos islands for the same reasons the diving is exalted (see above). This is a great place to learn to snorkel—the waters are clean, clear, temperate, and gentle—and the marine life is rich and thriving.

A number of watersports operators offer snorkeling trips (or combination snorkeling/beach excursions) off Grace Bay or in and around
the Caicos Cays, a short (30-min.) trip from Leeward Marina (see
"Caicos Watersports Operators: Master List," above). **Caicos Adventures** takes you farther still, on 4.6m-wide (15-ft.) powered catamarans, to superb snorkeling spots in West Caicos and French Cay, both
about an hour's boat ride from Leeward (𝒞 **649/941-3346;** www.
caicosadventures.com).

You can even find great snorkeling opportunities right on Grace
Bay. While most resorts along Grace Bay offer complimentary snorkeling equipment with which you can happily tool around the clear
shallows in front of your hotel, it's unlikely that you'll see anything
other than the clear turquoise sea and a sprinkling of pink-tinged
sunrise tellins or sun-bleached coral. If you really want to see an active
underwater marine garden, grab your snorkeling equipment and head
down the beach to one of Grace Bay's two prime snorkeling spots,
Smith's Reef and **Bight Reef,** both in the Princess Alexandra
National Park, on Provo's northern coastline.

Smith's Reef, near Turtle Cove Marina, is a walk-in dive to a sea-
scape of brain and fan corals, purple gorgonians, anemones, sea
cucumbers, sergeant majors, green parrotfish, long-nosed trumpet
fish, the ominous-looking green moray, an occasional southern ray,
and a visiting hawksbill turtle or two. Smith's Reef has underwater
signs that describe the coral reef ecosystem and the diversity of life
that thrives there. Snorkelers can learn about the various creatures
camouflaged within the reef, the importance of sea-grass beds, and
the ways that parrotfish contribute to the environment. The trail fol-
lows the perimeter of the reef starting inshore in about 1 to 2m
(3¼–6½ ft.) of water, increasing to 7 to 9m (23–30 ft.) deep. The
depth marks a spectacular display of coral creations, colorful school-
ing fish, and spotted eagle rays; even resident turtles can be found.

Even closer than Smith's Reef to most guests staying on Grace
Bay, Bight Reef is located in the Grace Bay area known as the Bight,
just offshore Coral Gardens. A public footpath leads to the beach,
and two marker buoys indicate both ends of the snorkel trail. The
Bight Reef Snorkel Trail has underwater trail signs that describe
corals and how they grow. Water depth ranges from 1 to 5m (3¼–16
ft.), and visitors can view mobile species like yellowtail snappers, big
jolthead porgies, and sand-sifting mojarras. You can get snorkeling
equipment (and even diving lessons) at **Cactus Voyager,** the in-
house dive operator in Coral Gardens resort, directly in front of the
reef (𝒞 **649/941-3713**).

On **North Caicos** the snorkeling is especially good at Three Mary Cays, a marine sanctuary just east of Sandy Point and part of 11km-long (7-mile) Whitby Beach. On **Middle Caicos** you can snorkel in Mudjin Harbor around Dragon Cay.

3 BEACH EXCURSIONS & BOAT CHARTERS

One of the most popular watersports activities in the Provo area is a **beach excursion ★★** offered by a number of charter-boat operators. These excursions come in any number of variations and combinations, and in many instances you can personally tailor your own excursion or hire a private charter to take you to a secluded cay for the day.

Charter boats no longer leave out of Leeward Marina (it's now the Nikki Beach resort complex) but from Heaving Down Rock marina, on Provo's northeast shore—and most operators include hotel or resort pickup and drop-off in the price of your excursion.

A favorite beach excursion is a half-day or full day out on the Caicos Cays that includes **snorkeling, a visit to Iguana Island** (see box), and a **shelling stopover** on one of the uninhabited cays. Other variations include **conch diving** (you can try to dive the 6m/20-ft. depths, but most people let the expert guides do the diving to retrieve fresh conch) and a subsequent lunch of fresh conch salad, prepared on the spot ceviche-style; **beach barbecues or picnics;** or **sunset cruises** with wine and cheese.

On a **glowworm cruise,** boats take you out around sunset 4 or 5 days after a full moon to see millions of mating glowworms light up the shallow local waters with a glittering green glow.

More ambitious beach excursions include **"island safaris"** and **eco-tours** in North or Middle Caicos, trips that may combine boating and snorkeling with caving, bird-watching, kayaking, biking, hiking, visiting historic sites, or having lunch in a native home. **Big Blue Unlimited** (© 649/946-5034; www.bigblueunlimited.com) is highly recommended for its creative eco-tours.

A number of watersports operators offer **private charters,** whether for personalized island touring or just a pickup or drop-off on another island.

For contact information on recommended operators who offer excellent beach excursions and private charters, go to the "Caicos Watersports Operators: Master List," earlier in this chapter.

A Visit to Iguana Island

Many of the beach excursions to the Caicos Cays include a
short tour of **Little Water Cay** ★, a protected nature reserve
(part of the Princess Alexandra National Park) and home to
the **Turks and Caicos rock iguana,** a small, harmless reptile
that is found nowhere else on the planet. Boardwalks and
observation towers have been constructed at two popular
landing sites to reduce the impact of tourism—this is, after all,
one of the most popular attractions in the Turks and Caicos.
As you walk along the wooden boardwalks that crisscross the
47-hectare (116-acre) island, you'll spot members of the island
iguana population, here some 3,000 strong, emerging from
their sand burrows. The biggest of these iguanas are more
than .6m (2 ft.) long and solid; they're handsome fellows, if
you like the rough-and-ready type, and rule the roost. The
rock iguanas of Turks and Caicos are the islands' largest native
land animal—even so, they're no match for a number of pred-
ators, including cats. About 50,000 rock iguanas remain here,
the largest and healthiest population in the Caribbean. A park
access fee of $5 per visitor is charged to help support further
conservation activities.

4 SAILING, PARASAILING & OTHER WATERSPORTS

KAYAKING   An increasingly popular activity on the TCI is kayaking. **Big Blue** (© **649/946-5034;** www.bigblue.tc) offers kayaking
eco-tours in the Caicos Cays, North Caicos, and Middle Caicos.

KITEBOARDING & WINDSURFING   Kiteboarding—also known
as kitesurfing—has really taken off on the Turks and Caicos. Conditions for this sport are excellent: The calms waters are protected by a
coral reef, the seas are uncrowded, and winds can be very cooperative.
You can get kiteboarding and windsurfing lessons and/or equipment
rentals directly on Grace Bay beach from **Windsurfing Provo** (in
front of the Ocean Club East resort; © **649/241-1687;** www.wind
surfingprovo.tc; Windsurfing rates are $40/hour and $150/day). Also
recommended is **KiteProvo** (© **649/242-2927;** www.kiteprovo.
com), with IKO- and PASA-certified instructors Mike Haas and Terri

Tapper. Both Windsurfing Provo and KiteProvo offer 3-hour Kite-boarding Fundamentals lessons for $225/per person an hour. **Big Blue** (© 649/946-5034; www.bigblue.tc) also offers windsurfing and kite-boarding expeditions, lessons, and rentals.

PARASAILING You won't see jet skis blazing across Grace Bay, but you will see billowy parasails skimming the clouds. It's a thrilling sight, the colorful parasails casting shadows on the aquamarine seas. Call on **Captain Marvin's Water Sports,** Grace Bay (© 649/231-0643; www.captainmarvinswatersports.com). A 15-minute flight over beautiful Grace Bay costs $75. You can also take a banana-boat ride at $25 per person or go water-skiing for $275 per hour ($250 per hour for more than 1 hr.).

SAILING Sailing excursions are offered by many charter groups, most notably **Sail Provo** (© 649/946-4783; www.sailprovo.com/contact. htm). It sails 14m or 15m (48-ft. or 52-ft.) catamarans on half- or full-day excursions. One of the most frequented is a sailing and snorkeling trip for $63 that's offered on Monday, Wednesday, and Saturday and includes a tour of Little Water Cay, or "Iguana Island." A full-day cruise Tuesday to Friday costs $124, including a lunch buffet served onboard. Sail Provo also offers sunset cruises and glowworm cruises.

A retired rumrunner, *Atabeyra*, is owned by **Sun Charters** (© 649/231-0624; www.suncharters.tc). Happy hour sunset cruises cost $39 per person. Customized private charters can be arranged for half- or

Spotting JoJo the Dolphin

JoJo, a wild Atlantic bottlenose dolphin, is a local celebrity here and acts like one, showing off for visitors as he plays in the waters of Grace Bay. He's even a movie star, having appeared in *Nature* and *In the Wild: Dolphins,* both PBS specials, and the 2000 IMAX film *Dolphins.* He's so famous he's been named a Turks & Caicos National Treasure and as such enjoys protected status. He likes to trail boats, and sightings of JoJo in the clear Grace Bay sea happen almost daily. A whole cottage industry of all things JoJo has sprung up. You can learn more about JoJo and the JoJo Project on the website of the **Marine Wildlife Foundation** (www.marinewildlife. org), which is dedicated to the research and preservation of dolphins, whales, and all marine life. A bell at Hemingway's on the Beach oceanfront restaurant at the Sands at Grace Bay resort is there for anyone to ring if they spot JoJo.

(Kids) Day Pass at Beaches

Even if you're not staying there, you can treat yourself and your family to a day's worth of all the resort activities, meals and drinks, and encounters with *Sesame Street* characters you can possibly stand with a day pass to the all-inclusive **Beaches Turks & Caicos Resort & Spa.** The cost is $200 per adult ($130 per child) and lasts from 9am until 5pm. It's an especially fun option for the small kids in your party who are gaga for all things Elmo and Cookie Monster—and not a bad day at the beach for older kids who have total access to Beaches' wealth of sports and watersports facilities—including the new Pirates Island Waterpark, with seven water slides, a lazy river, a waterfall pool, and surf simulator—and Xbox 360 Game Garage. Turn to chapter 3 for a rundown of all the activities that Beaches has to offer. For more information, call *©* **649/946-8000.**

full-day trips and include food, drinks, snorkeling gear, and sailing down the chain of Caicos Cays, perhaps following an ocean trail blazed by Columbus. A kid-pleasing 3-hour Pirate Cruise goes to Treasure Island and costs $49 to $59.

You can also sail aboard the catamaran *Beluga* (*©* **649/946-4396;** www.sailbeluga.com) where Captain Tim Ainley leads small, personally tailored beach excursions or private charters for romantic beach barbecues.

STAND-UP PADDLEBOARDING The Turks & Caicos have ideal conditions for stand-up paddleboarding, one of the fastest-growing board sports in the world. It's pretty much what the name implies: You are standing up on a thick surfboard and propelling yourself through the water with a long paddle. You cruise along in calm, flat waters along the shoreline or through peaceful mangrove channels. It's a total body workout—as well as a balancing act. **Big Blue,** always at the forefront of eco-sensitive activities, offers stand-up paddleboarding expeditions and rentals (*©* **649/946-5034;** www.bigblue.tc). (Parrot Cay also has stand-up paddleboards.)

5 FISHING

The fishing is excellent in the Turks and Caicos, whether bonefishing, reef fishing, deep-sea fishing, or bottom fishing. A number of reputable

(Kids) Kid Stuff

The 2010 arrival of **FunWorld,** a mini golf/go-cart/game arcade complex, was as inevitable as the summer rain. It avoids being a total beach-resort cliché by throwing in savory grilled jerk chicken and live music on the weekends—and, we admit, it's great family fun. The newest attraction in Provo is at corner of the East Leeward Highway and Long Bay Road (© **649/941-4659;** www.funworldtci.com). The 18-hole minia-ture golf course is $15 adults and $10 children 10 and under.

boat-charter companies offer fishing expeditions; go to the "Caicos Watersports Operators: Master List," earlier in this chapter for con-tact information. **Silver Deep** (© **649/941-5441;** www.silverdeep. com) offers fishing excursions, with both half- and full-day expedi-tions, usually for bonefishing or bottom fishing. Tackle and bait are included.

For those who'd like to venture farther afield—and pay a lot more money—half- and full-day deep-sea fishing expeditions are available, with all equipment included. Catches turn up wahoo, tuna, kingfish, marlin, and even shark.

In Middle Caicos, **Cardinal Arthur** (© **649/946-6107;** cellphone 649/241-0730) is a one-man fishing charter. The sixth-generation Middle Caicos native can take you fishing for snapper, grouper, grunt, or barracuda.

6 GOLF & TENNIS

From a country that currently has only two golf courses (on Provo and Grand Turk), the TCI golf scene is somewhat limited. However, rumors persist that the Northwest Point area will get a golf course in the near future.

GOLF Provo Golf & Country Club ★, on Grace Bay Road (© **649/946-5833;** www.provogolfclub.com), is one of only two golf courses in the country (the other is on Grand Turk). The 6,560-yard, par-72, 18-hole course was designed by Karl Litten of Boca Raton, Florida, and is owned by the Turks and Caicos Water Company. It is powerfully green and—because Provo is one of the driest spots on the globe—it takes an extraordinary amount of water to keep it that way. Young palms and bougainvillea, as well as rocky outcroppings and powdery sand traps, help make the course a challenge to the serious golfer or a lovely day on the links for the beginner or novice. Four sets of tees allow golfers to tailor a game to their level of expertise. A driving range and putting greens are also available. Inside the newly renovated clubhouse is a full-service restaurant and bar called **Fairways Bar & Grill** (p. 93).

Greens fees are $165 per person for 18 holes. The price includes the use of a shared golf cart, which is mandatory. Golf clubs can be rented for $30 to $60 per set. The course is open from 7am to 7:30pm daily. The course also has two lighted hard tennis courts (see below). Inside the clubhouse is the Pro Shop, a fully stocked store with golf and tennis equipment as well as tennis and golf shoes, collared shirts, tailored shorts, and hats.

TENNIS   Many of Provo's hotels and resorts have on-site tennis courts, including Beaches, Club Med, the Grace Bay Club, the Ocean Club, the Palms, and the Sands at Grace Bay. The **Provo Golf & Country Club** has two lighted hard courts that the public is welcome to reserve ($10 per person per hour; reserve 24 hr. in advance; open daily 7am–7:30pm).

Pamela Ewing's Favorite TCI Experiences

Pamela Ewing is a Belonger (a native-born Turks islander) who knows just about anyone and everyone on the islands—which makes her job working for the Turks & Caicos Tourist Board a perfect fit. Like most Turks and Caicos Islanders, Pamela puts great stock in hanging out with family and friends over food in a laid-back atmosphere. Here are Pamela's favorite TCI experiences:

- Going to the **Children's Park** on Lower Bight Road on Grace Bay with the kids and enjoying the beach and a good picnic or a cookout, with local foods such as conch fritters, fish with rice and vegetables, or souse (chicken).
- Going to the **caves** on Middle Caicos and doing a cave safari on a day trip. This involves an all-day boat trip to Middle Caicos. On the way you can swim and snorkel and then you visit the caves and have lunch.
- **Fishing off the docks.**
- Visiting **North Caicos,** to places like Wades Green. It's best to take a boat, rather than a plane.

It's been reported that a deal has been signed to bring a **NASCAR raceway** to the Blue Hills of Provo. Whether the deal goes through or not is anyone's guess, but if it does, the raceway is expected to host seasonal events and not ongoing races.

PROVIDENCIALES

Provo has little in the way of historic or cultural attractions; for a real feel for the rich heritage of the TCI, you'll need to head to North or Middle Caicos (see below) and, of course, to Grand Turk and Salt Cay (see chapter 6).

At press time, it was not clear if the **Caicos Conch Farm** in Provo was up and running again after suffering severe damage in the hurricanes of 2008. Call ✆ **649/946-5330** to see if the attraction (and working conch farm) has opened and is offering tours.

Cheshire Hall   Many of the Belongers who live on these islands are descendants of slaves brought here by British Loyalists in the 18th century to build and work vast cotton plantations. Cheshire Hall was built by a Loyalist named Wade Stubbs from Cheshire County, England. He and his brother William grew sea-island cotton on thousands of acres of land until the crop was exhausted in the early 19th century. The ruins of the Great House sit atop a lush, overgrown hill, surrounded by the crumbling remains of outbuildings, once-bustling engines to the cotton trade. The Turks & Caicos National Trust runs guided tours Monday to Friday 8:30am to 4pm; call to arrange a tour.

Off Leeward Hwy., Providenciales. ✆ **649/941-5710.** www.nationaltrust.tc. Tours $5 per person.

NORTH CAICOS

A number of charter-boat operators offer island tours, eco-tours, bird-watching tours, or private charters to North Caicos, including **Big Blue Unlimited** (✆ **649/946-5034;** www.bigblueunlimited.com). Big Blue combines boat rides with bike trips, kayaking, bird-watching, and lunches in native homes to get deep into the North Caicos experience. You many even get to **Flamingo Pond,** tidal flats on the island's south side and home to the largest protected nature sanctuary of West Indian flamingos in the islands.

Wades Green Plantation   North Caicos became plantation country when Americans loyal to the British crown (Loyalists) fled the United States to come here, where they were provided property from the British crown, in the wake of the War of Independence. According to historians at the Turks & Caicos National Museum, in

1788 the Caicos islands had a population of over 40 white families and 1,200 slaves. All slaves were freed in 1834, and today many descendants of these slaves reside in North Caicos. The main industry on these plantations was growing sea-island cotton, an endeavor that eventually failed as a result of dry conditions, thin soil, pests, and tropical storms. Today you can still see the occasional cotton plant growing tall along the roadside in both North and Middle Caicos. Outside of Kew are the ruins of one of the most successful plantations of the Loyalist era, Wades Green, which was constructed by Florida Loyalist Wade Stubbs around 1789 and eventually grew to 1,214 hectares (3,000 acres). Today you can see the ruins of the stone house, outbuildings, and surrounding walls, pillowed in North Caicos scrub brush. Call the Turks & Caicos National Trust for tours.

Kew, North Caicos. ℭ **649/946-5710.** tc.natrust@tciway.tc.

MIDDLE CAICOS

Big Blue Unlimited (ℭ **649/946-5034;** www.bigblueunlimited. com) combines boat rides with bike trips, kayaking, swimming, and cave exploration on Middle Caicos. Middle Caicos native and guide **Cardinal Arthur** (ℭ **649/946-6107;** cellphone 649/241-0730) offers cave, bird-watching, fishing, and eco-tours, transportation, and general sightseeing trips of the island. Also offering cave tours (and good general sightseeing tours) is local guide **Ernest Forbes, Sr.** (ℭ **649/946-6140**).

Conch Bar Caves National Park ★ These cool limestone caves are a surprising treat to discover on flat, sunbaked TCI. This massive (24km/15-mile) aboveground limestone cave system (with 3.2km/2 miles of surveyed caves) was used by pre-Columbian Lucayan Indians more than 600 years ago—a number of artifacts from their occupation are housed in the Turks & Caicos National Museum. Today it's basically a big bat cave (mined for exported guano back in the late 19th c.), with impressive stalactites, stalagmites, flowstone, and pools. Look for land crabs around the entrance to the caves. *Tip:* Spray yourself thoroughly with mosquito repellent before you go in. For more information, contact the **Turks & Caicos National Trust** (ℭ **649/946-5710**).

The Crossing Place Trail ★ This historic coastal route, much of it along a bluff overlooking the lovely azure waters of Mudjin Harbor, was first established in the late 1700s by cotton plantation settlers. As part of the Turks & Caicos National Trust Middle Caicos Ecotourism Project, it has been reopened from the Conch Bar to the Indian Cave field road. (Crossing Place refers to the place where in years past people crossed the sandbars at low tide to get to North Caicos.) During the days of the Loyalist plantations, the owners rode along the

King's Road while the slaves walked the trail. You can hike or bike this trail; go to **www.tcimall.tc/middlecaicos/crossingplace.htm** for more information on hiking and biking routes. The trail is generally flat, with some low hills. For more information, contact the **Turks & Caicos National Trust** (© 649/946-5710).

8 SPAS & GYMS

The resorts of Providenciales and the Caicos Cays have some of the finest spas in the Caribbean region—and for many, you don't even have to be a guest to take advantage of some truly splendid treatments. (You'll need to reserve any spa treatment in advance, of course.)

If you don't want to go the resort route, we recommend the spa treatments at **Spa Tropique** (© 649/231-6938; www.spatropique. com; hours vary), which has several locations on Grace Bay (in the Sands at Grace Bay resort and the Ports of Call shopping plaza) and even makes house calls—try its Body Tropique product line, made with local ingredients like sea salt.

Here is a sampling of some of the top resort spas in the TCI that welcome nonguests. Be sure to ask whether a service charge has been added to the bill automatically (some places automatically tack on service charges up to 18%).

ANANI SPA   This is the Grace Bay Club's full-service spa, and it already boasts some of the top massage therapists on the island. The spa specializes in Euro-Asian spa techniques, and treatments range from "aroma stone therapy" to deep-tissue massage to ocean wraps. You can get a treatment in one of the six indoor treatment rooms or outdoors in one of two beach spa tents. Massages cost from $80 to $165; the spa is open daily from 9am to 7pm (6pm in summer). Call **649/946-5050,** ext. 1045, for appointments.

COMO SHAMBHALA   Many people think this is the finest spa in the Caribbean, and it's hard to argue otherwise. The 613-sq.-m (6,600-sq.-ft.) space at the Parrot Cay resort is wrapped in a sea of glass that looks out over the island wetlands. Inside several freestanding wooden pavilions are treatment salons where Eastern-influenced healing and rejuvenating therapies are applied by Balinese healers. The spa has both a yoga studio and a Pilates studio, as well as an outdoor Jacuzzi garden outside the women's locker room.

EXHALE SPA   Bringing big-city spa treatments to Provo, Exhale Spa (www.exhalespa.com) at the Gansevoort Turks + Caicos offers

Day Tripping on Parrot Cay

You can enjoy the superlative spa experience at COMO Shambhala (above) by arranging a **day trip** to the island. The cost for the boat transfer is $100 per person, and you can eat lunch in the Lotus restaurant or enjoy the lovely beach or the pool while you're there—the costs of food, tips, and spa treatments are on you, of course. Call ✆ **649/946-7788** (http://shambhala.como.bz) to reserve a treatment and arrange a boat transfer, which leaves out of the resort's own dock at Leeward. Massages run from $150 to $240.

fusion massage, couples' massage, deep tissue massage, body scrubs, as well as facials, manicures, pedicures, and brow and body waxing. Call ✆ **649/941-7555** for reservations. Massages run from $115 to $330.

THE REGENT SPA AT THE REGENT PALMS You'll feel better just stepping into this place, which is elegant and soothing all at once. It's simply a beautiful space, classically designed around reflecting pools. Some of the treatment rooms are set in alfresco coral-stone cabanas shaded by palm trees. The menu of services is extensive and includes facials, massages, body scrubs and other therapies, and day retreat packages (the Regent Palms resort, Grace Bay, Providenciales; ✆ **649/946-8666,** ext. 30208 or 30211; www.regenthotels.com/the palms). Massages run from $80 to $215; it's open daily from 8am to 8pm.

THE THALASSO SPA AT POINT GRACE The ambience is absolutely dreamy: outdoors in an open-air structure with beach views and sea breezes. This full-service oceanfront European-style thalassotherapy spa uses the properties of seawater as well as applications of sea mud and select seaweed in its body and facial treatments. The menu includes Swedish massage, shiatsu, body scrubs, and wraps (Point Grace Resort, Providenciales; ✆ **649/946-5096,** ext. 4126). Open daily from 9am to 6pm. Massages start at $75.

GYMS

Many resorts have on-site gyms or fitness centers. For those that don't, **Pulse Gym** (the Saltmills, Grace Bay Rd.; ✆ **649/941-8686**) is open 7 days a week and has Cybex strength and cardio equipment; free weights; and exercise, Pilates, and yoga classes.

Shopping the Hotel Boutiques

Shopping doesn't have to stop at your hotel door. A number of hotels and resorts in Provo have very good in-house boutique shops, many selling items you won't find in most standard-issue hotel gift shops. Here are a few recommended shops and a sampling of the goods you might discover there:

- **Amanyara:** This hotel resort on Provo's Northwest Point offers such high-end goodies as Asian-inspired tunic tops by Elizabeth Hurley Beach; Havaianas flip-flops from Brazil; and Amanresorts' wonderful spa products.
- **Beaches:** Beaches has two stores: **Treasure Island,** which sells high-end beachwear, Beaches-branded T-shirts, hats, and beach paraphernalia, gifts, snacks, soft drinks, and limited toiletries; and **Pirate Cove,** which sells *Sesame Street*–branded clothes and toys and other kids' items.
- **The Gansevoort:** Not surprisingly for this cosmopolitan brand, this boutique sells sexy (and pricey) styles in swimwear and silky kurtas, among other high-end products.
- **The Meridian Club:** This small shop sells Meridian Club T-shirts, tops, and hats, locally crafted basketry, and other gift items.
- **The Palms:** Palm Place, which faces the terrace of restaurant Parallel23, is a real shopping mecca, featuring not one

9 SHOPPING

Providenciales and the Caicos islands are still a work in progress when it comes to shopping, although an increasing number of small shopping "villages" or plazas have cropped up along Grace Bay Road including the **Ocean Club Plaza, Regent Village,** and **Le Vele plaza.** The older shopping plazas are the **Saltmills** (Grace Bay Rd.), which has seven shops, including a wine-and-liquor store, and several restaurants; and **Ports of Call** (Grace Bay Rd.), with eight shops and several restaurants.

You may not be shopping until you drop during your TCI vacation, but you can discover some real gems if you do some digging—particularly when it comes to regional artwork, much of it reasonably priced and including the famously colorful paintings by artists from but five boutique shops. **Wish** boutique has upscale clothing, including those sweet little soft cotton tops and skirts from designer James Perse. Next door the **Palm Shop** carries casual logo wear and gift items. **Splash** has beachwear. **Spice** has gourmet snacks and beverages, such as Harry and David chocolate-covered cherries and Miss Vickie's Potato Chips. **Harmony Gallery** sells lots of the home furnishings and pricey little tchotchkes (handblown-glass conch shells, sea-urchin candlesticks, shell-encrusted mirrors) you see around the hotel. (Oh, and you can also buy skin-care products and treatments along with big-ticket yoga- and sleepwear in the **Spa at the Palms.**)

• **Parrot Cay:** The shop sells lovely but pricey jewel-encrusted Asian-style tunics and kurtas, along with other high-end clothing, books, jewelry, bags, and a few essential toiletries. The COMO Shambhala spa's wildly popular Invigorate line of soaps, shampoos, and the like is also on sale here.

• **Somerset on Grace Bay:** This nice little boutique is packed with goodies such as Sita de Vesci beachwear, silk kurtas, Theory clothing, jewelry, bathing suits, and menswear.

neighboring Haiti, as well as local crafts, such as beautifully made Middle Caicos fanner-grass baskets and silvertop-palm bags, hats, and other items.

Most shops are open from 9 or 10am to 5 or 6pm (generally later in the high season), but hours are ultimately subject to the owners' whims. Be sure to call in advance so you aren't disappointed to find that a store has shut down for the day.

ARTWORK

Art Provo ★   In its new location, this art gallery has a large selection of paintings by local artists, Turks and Caicos pottery, baskets, jewelry, and glass. Look for local painters like Dwight Outten (cousin to Phillip; see below), a Middle Caicos native whose clean-lined, realistic oil paintings of the region are particularly fine. Also represented are artists Laura Lancaster, Heather Forbes, and Jill Segal.

Regent Village, Grace Bay Rd., Providenciales. ✆ **649/941-4545.** www.art provo.com.

Maison Creole   This shop has some lovely Haitian arts and crafts, including hand-painted place mats and boxes. Maison Creole closed its shop on Grace Bay Road but still has a small shop in the international-departures lounge at the Provo airport. International Departures Lounge, Providenciales International Airport, Providenciales. ✆ **649/946-4285.**

BOOKS

Unicorn Bookstore   This, the island's only full-service bookstore, has books (bestsellers, fiction, nonfiction, kids' books, and more), newspapers, magazines, and gifts. It also has a second, smaller location on Grace Bay Road, in the Ports of Call shopping plaza. Leeward Hwy., in front of the IGA Graceway, Providenciales. ✆ **649/941-5458.**

CLOTHING

Caicos Wear   This small clothing store offers a good selection of comfortable casual wear, sundresses, colorful peasant skirts, bathing suits, and bags. La Petite Place, Grace Bay Rd., Grace Bay. ✆ **649/941-3346.**

Dive Provo   This dive operator's shop offers dive trips and snorkeling equipment, plus some surprisingly stylish casual tops and shorts that work well in a tropical clime. Ports of Call shopping plaza, Grace Bay Rd., Providenciales. ✆ **649/946-5040.** www.diveprovo.com.

GIFTS/HOME FURNISHINGS

Belongings   This home-furnishings store meshes a sleek urban design sensibility with breezy island inspirations. You'll find lots you'll want to take home here: from beautiful lamps with mother-of-pearl mosaic bases and reproduced antique book plates to simple, elegant table linens, vases, candleholders, and reversible quilts. Ports of Call shopping plaza. ✆ **649/941-8055.** http://belongingstc.com.

HANDICRAFTS

Middle Caicos Co-op ★★   Handsome hand-carved model Caicos islands sailing sloops can be custom-ordered from the Middle Caicos Co-op—sail plan, size, and color schemes all to your specifications. These sloops are carved from the native gum-elemi tree, a Caribbean softwood. The co-op also sells fanner-grass baskets, silver-top-palm straw hats, bags, and more, plus Middle Caicos grits. Conch Bar, Middle Caicos. ✆/fax **649/946-6132.** www.tcimall.tc/middlecaicos/co-op.htm or e-mail middlecaicos@tciway.tc.

Turks & Caicos National Trust Shop ★   Here you can find the real deal: crafts and products made in the Turks and Caicos, including native pottery, fanner-grass baskets, silvertop-palm bags, model

Caicos sloops, and more. Get your rock iguana T-shirts here! Grace
Bay Plaza, Grace Bay Rd., Providenciales. (C) **649/941-3536.** www.national trust.tc.

JEWELRY

Jai's   This duty-free shop sells a number of big international brands, including Cartier, Bulgari, David Yurman, Movado, and Tag Heuer. It also has locations in the international-departures lounge in the Provo airport and in the Grand Turk Cruise Center. Regent Village, Grace Bay Rd., Providenciales. (C) **649/941-4324.** www.jais.tc.

10 NIGHTLIFE

The nightlife on Provo can't compete with the late-night revelry of, say, Aruba or even Barbados. The TCI is a fairly conservative place, overall. This is a laid-back kind of place with laid-back pleasures, but it does offer a number of quality nighttime diversions.

BEACH SHACKS

The **beach shacks along Blue Hills Beach** are great places to drink Turk's Head beer or a little rum, eat conch, and listen to good music. On Wednesday nights, Smokey's on the Bay has a popular Wednesday-night fish fry.

CASINOS

The casino action has picked up with the emergence of two casinos. The **Casablanca Casino** offers roulette, blackjack, craps, and baccarat and is open from 1pm to 5am (Grace Bay Rd., Providenciales; (C) **649/941-3737**).

LOUNGES/BARS/SPORTS BARS

BEACHSIDE BARS   Providenciales has some terrific beachside lounges or bars from which you can watch the sunset. Two of the best are the Grace Bay Club's **Lounge,** with white-cushion seating and glowing fire pit, and sister lounge the **Infinity Bar,** which has the longest bar in the Caribbean: a sleek ribbon of black marble inset with sexy blue lights ((C) **649/946-5050**). The **Beach Lounge** at the Gansevoort is an attractive new gathering spot, and the resort's **Bagatelle Bistrot** ((C) **649/941-7555**) has DJ nights, dancing, and happy hours. Also visit the bar/lounge/deck at **Amanyara** ((C) **649/941-8133**), the **Plunge** pool bar (the Palms resort; (C) **649/946-8666**), and any of the **Blue Hills beach shacks** (see the "Dining Da Blue Hills" sidebar, in chapter 4).

GOLF COURSE BAR   The **Fairways Bar** at the Provo Golf & Country Club (✆ **649/946-5833**) is a pleasant place to have a drink and munch on hearty bar food.

IRISH PUB   **Danny Buoy's** (Grace Bay Rd., Providenciales; ✆ **649/946-5921**) features a full bar stocked with imported beers on tap, darts, and pool tables; it also has ESPN-U, for hard-core college sports fans. Danny Buoy's has good food, with dishes from across the pond (bangers and mash, Irish stew) as well as island fare (jerk chicken).

LIVE MUSIC   Most of the island's bars, hotels, and restaurants feature live-music nights. Look for the talented duo NaDa on the O'Soleil terrace at the Somerset Resort most Saturdays. Turks Islander Stanley Roots plays reggae at the Alexandra resort's sunset cookouts. Hemingway's has live music 3 nights a week. Check the local listings for updated schedules.

MARINA BARS   **Turtle Cove Marina** in the northwest section of Provo has a good number of jolly, atmospheric dockside bars, many with happy hours (5–7pm); all serve food, both bar snacks and full-service menus. Join in the revelry at **Baci** (✆ **649/941-3044**), **Banana Boat** (✆ **649/941-5706**), the **Tiki Hut Cabana Bar** (✆ **649/941-5341**), and the **Sharkbite Bar & Grill** (✆ **649/941-5090**). Up above Turtle Cove, at the Miramar Resort, is the **Magnolia Wine Bar** (✆ **649/941-5108**), a lounge next to the Magnolia restaurant with bird's-eye views of Provo and the Grace Bay shoreline. **Gilley's** (✆ **649/946-5094**), at **Leeward Marina,** has a full bar with both indoor and terrace seating as well as a full-service restaurant serving good island cuisine (including Gilley's Famous Local Grouper Sandwich). Gilley's also has a branch at the Provo airport.

SPORTS BARS   **Club Sodax** is a nice sports bar with a good mix of locals and tourists (Leeward Hwy., Providenciales; ✆ **649/941-4540**). **Bambooz Bar & Grill** (at the Saltmills shopping plaza, Grace Bay Rd., Providenciales; ✆ **649/941-8146**) is another popular spot where you can watch sports on big-screen plasma TVs, listen to music, or dine on island fare or international cuisine.

MOVIE THEATERS

L'Raye Cinemas, the islands' only movie theater, opened in Provo in late 2007 with three screens. It was named for the former first lady of the TCI, Hollywood actress LisaRaye McCoy Misick. It's located on Leeward Highway.

The Turks Islands: Grand Turk & Salt Cay

If you think Providenciales is laid-back, prepare yourself for the *really* relaxed worlds of Grand Turk and Salt Cay. Grand Turk and Salt Cay are low-key charmers that hold quaint architectural remnants of the islands' colonial past. If you love to scuba dive or snorkel, have a thing for sun-drenched beaches and ridiculously beautiful seas, and crave a relaxed, back-to-basics departure from the chichi boutique-resort scene, a visit to both islands during your vacation is highly recommended.

1 GRAND TURK ★★

Note: Grand Turk continues to recover from a devastating direct hit by Hurricane Ike in September 2008, which left a good percentage of the island's structures damaged or destroyed, including some historic properties. The island's lodgings are open for business, however (see below), and the surrounding coral reef and undersea "Wall" are reportedly recovering as well, good news for divers and snorkelers who make pilgrimages here from around the globe to explore Grand Turk's spectacular marine waters.

Grand Turk is the capital of the Turks and Caicos Islands, although it is no longer the financial and business hub of the island nation, having lost that position to Provo. It is no longer the transportation hub either, as Provo receives 95% of the international airplane landings. The island is rather barren and wind-swept, and even though lovely green bluffs top its northwest and eastern shores, don't come here looking for lush tropical foliage. Do consider Grand Turk, however, if you want a destination that's excellent for snorkeling and diving, with beautiful white-sand beaches and a friendly, small-town vibe. You might say it's Mayberry by the Sea.

Cockburn Town (*Coe*-burn) is the financial and business center of this tiny (11×3.2km/7×2 miles) island. The best place for swimming is **Governor's Beach** near the governor's residence, **Waterloo,** on the

The Day the Cruise Ships Came to Town

Grand Turk is the kind of place that lingers with you long after you've left. Maybe that's why some people were concerned that the new kids in town—the Carnival Cruise Line ships that started arriving at the **Grand Turk Cruise Center** in February 2006—would rend the very fabric that makes this place unique. In a 40-year land-lease deal with the TCI government, the cruise line has built a $42-million "tourism village" designed to look like a Bermudian salt-rakers' settlement from the early 19th century. It's a colorful representation of the local architecture, but its theme-park underpinnings can't help but peek through. Jimmy Buffett's Margaritaville, for example, is here, bigger, bolder, and brassier than any other Margaritaville on earth, straddled by a lagoon pool with swim-up bars and slides. And silliness reigns when cruise passengers driving multicolored dune buggies parade through the streets of Grand Turk.

Carnival did many wonderful things for Grand Turk in preparation for its opening. It paved the potholed Duke Street area and sandblasted the dirt off the old lighthouse. It brought construction jobs and spiffier taxis to the islands, and locally owned shops opened up in the cruise center. It's bringing business to local tour operators, and a nice touch is the horse-drawn carriages that clip-clop through town. On the downside, it cut a hole (said to be an environmentally

west coast of the island. Take time to tour Cockburn Town's **historic section,** particularly Duke and Front streets, where 200-year-old structures crafted of wood and limestone line the waterfront. Stroll the area and soak in the rhythms of Cockburn Town, the vintage architecture behind picket fences entwined with crimson bougainvillea, the fragrant trees, the funky beachfront bars, the wet suits hanging out to dry. Stay for a couple of days, and you'll be waving to familiar faces on the street, calling the local dogs by name, and settling into your new favorite spot on Duke Street to watch the sunset over a cool Turk's Head beer.

sensitive one but a hole nonetheless) in the coral reef to build a passage to allow 2,000- to 3,000-passenger ships to dock here.

The idea that a projected half-million visitors would descend on little Grand Turk annually has been a cause for concern, particularly among the diving community—the fear being that the presence of cruise ships would foment a slick, über-commercial tourism environment that could undermine the quirky, small-town charm and drive away former visitors. Only time will tell, but for the most part the cruise center at Grand Turk has been an unqualified success as well as a source of economic relief for a battered and beleaguered island, still in recovery from a brutal Category 5 hurricane and the global recession. Nearly 90% of the shops in the center are open, locals have opened restaurants and food stands nearby, and tour operators have jumped on the bandwagon with a range of shore excursions. In March 2008 Grand Turk won *Porthole Cruise Magazine*'s award for "The Most Unspoiled Caribbean Destination." And the cruise center is set far enough away from the center of Cockburn Town that the lovely, laid-back rhythms of Grand Turk continue apace.

For more on the cruise center, see "Exploring the Island," later in this chapter.

ESSENTIALS
VISITOR INFORMATION

The **Turks & Caicos Tourist Board** (www.turksandcaicostourism.com) has an office in Grand Turk (Front St., Cockburn Town; © **649/ 946-2321**). Office hours are Monday to Friday from 8:30am to 4:30pm.

Getting to Grand Turk

Your most likely point of entry into the Turks and Caicos Islands will be the **Providenciales International Airport** (www.provoairport. com; p. 31). To get to Grand Turk or Salt Cay, you will be taking a **domestic flight** on one of the interisland airlines (see below) or a charter plane from the Provo airport into Grand Turk International Airport (also known as J.A.G.S. McCartney International Airport). Several daily flights between Provo and Grand Turk are offered by **Air**

Turks & Caicos (✆ **649/946-4999** or 649/946-1667 on Grand Turk; www.airturksandcaicos.com). The flight from Provo to Grand Turk takes 25 minutes and costs $135 to $160 round-trip.

Getting around Grand Turk

On Grand Turk you can rent cars (as well as scooters, bicycles, and snorkeling gear) at **Tony's Car Rental** (Grand Turk International Airport; ✆ **649/964-1979;** www.tonyscarrental.com). Cars and jeeps rent for from $70 to $95 a day, scooter rentals cost $40 a day, and bike rentals are $20 a day. Tony's also offers scooter tours of the island.

Taxis are available, but there is no central agency to call. Your hotel can summon one for you, but taxis are always available at the Grand Turk airport. The fare is $10 to $12 from the airport to most inns and resorts. Drivers are more than happy to give visitors a tour of the island; expect to pay around $50 to $60 for a 45-minute island tour.

The **Grand Turk Experience** (✆ **649/246-5310**) is a bus that shuttles between the cruise terminal and the downtown area and also offers Grand Turk tours.

(*Fast Facts* Grand Turk

Area Code The area/country code for the TCI is **649.**

ATMs & ABMs **FirstCaribbean** has 24-hour ABM service at its main branch on Grand Turk. **Scotiabank** has a 24-hour ATM at Waterloo Plaza on Grand Turk. **TCI Bank Limited (TCIB)** has an ATM on Grand Turk.

Banks Branches and ATMs of **FirstCaribbean International Bank** (✆ **649/946-4245;** www.firstcaribbeanbank.com) and **Scotiabank** (✆ **649/946-4750;** www.scotiabank.com) are at convenient and central locations on Grand Turk. The country's first indigenous bank, **TCI Bank Limited (TCIB),** has opened a branch on Grand Turk.

Emergencies Call ✆ **649/946-2299** if you need the police.

Hospitals & Medical Facilities In April 2010, **Turks & Caicos Island Hospital,** the nation's first modern hospital, opened its two centers, one of which is the **Cockburn Town Medical Center** on Grand Turk. **Grand Turk Hospital** is on Hospital Road in Grand Turk (✆ **649/946-2040**).

Internet Access You can access the Internet at the small Internet cafe at **Mr. Cee's Supermarket** (Pond Rd.; ✆ **649/946-2995**), or try your hotel. Costs are typically around $10 an hour.

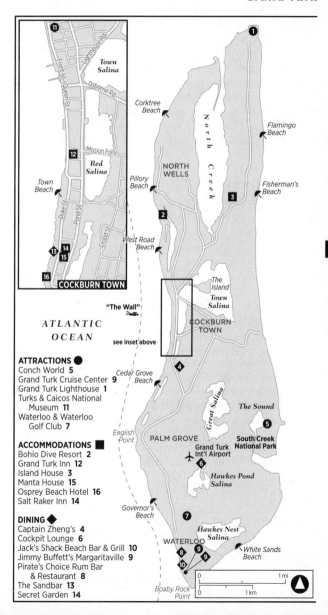

ATTRACTIONS ●
Conch World **5**
Grand Turk Cruise Center
Grand Turk Lighthouse **1**
Turks & Caicos National
  Museum **11**
Waterloo & Waterloo
  Golf Club **7**

ACCOMMODATIONS ■
Bohio Dive Resort **2**
Grand Turk Inn **12**
Island House **3**
Manta House **15**
Osprey Beach Hotel **16**
Salt Raker Inn **14**

DINING ◆
Captain Zheng's **4**
Cockpit Lounge **6**
Jack's Shack Beach Bar & Grill **10**
Jimmy Buffett's Margaritaville **9**
Pirate's Choice Rum Bar
  & Restaurant **8**
The Sandbar **13**
Secret Garden **14**

Language The official language is English.

Post Office The Grand Turk Post Office (© **649/946-1334**) is located in Cockburn Town. It's open Monday to Friday from 8am to 4pm.

Taxes There is a departure tax of $35, payable when you leave the islands (it's often included in the cost of your airfare). The government collects an 11% occupancy tax, applicable to all hotels, guesthouses, and restaurants in the 40-island chain. Resorts often add a 10% to 15% service charge on top of the government tax.

WHERE TO STAY
Hotels, Resorts & Inns

Most hotels add a 10% to 15% service charge, plus an 11% government occupancy tax, to the rates quoted below. Also keep in mind that many of the following resorts have a minimum-stay requirement during the winter high season.

Bohio Dive Resort ★   This resort has a splendid location directly overlooking beautiful Pillory Beach, the very spot where some historians believe Christopher Columbus first made landfall during his 1492 voyage to the New World. The main focus here is the hotel's in-house dive operation, with on-site PADI instructors and dive masters. Each of the serviceable 12 rooms and four suites, located in a separate building from the main section of the resort, has its own balcony with sea views; the suites have kitchenettes. The resort restaurant, **Guanahani,** serves breakfast, lunch, and dinner daily; the menu includes local favorites like conch chowder as well as standard Continental fare such as steaks and pasta—they'll even cook your day's catch for you. Or you can sample the bar menu, with burgers, fish, and conch (offered daily all day long) over a specialty Bohio cocktail at the convivial **Ike and Donkey Beach Bar,** built on the site of the original dive shack, which was blown away by Hurricane Ike in 2008. The hotel offers 3- to 7-night dive/stay packages; check the website for the latest rates.

Front St. (P.O. Box 179), Grand Turk, Turks and Caicos, B.W.I. © **649/946-2135.** Fax 649/946-1536. www.bohioresort.com. 16 units. Winter $190 double, $225 suite; off-season $165 double, $195 suite. Children 2 and under stay free in parent's room; children 3–12 stay for $35 extra a night. AE, MC, V. **Amenities:** Restaurant; bar; bikes; dive instructors and dive shack; excursions; outdoor pool; watersports equipment; Wi-Fi (in restaurant and bar; free). *In room:* A/C, ceiling fan, TV, kitchenette (in suites), fridge (in doubles), hair dryer.

Grand Turk Inn ★★ These are the best accommodations in Grand Turk. Sisters Katrina Birt and Sandy Erb, veterans of the Key West inn scene, discovered the charms of Grand Turk and the excellent bones of this handsome Bermudian-style 150-year-old former Methodist manse, which they lovingly renovated. The five suites are spacious and ultracomfortable, with king- or queen-size beds dressed in soft linens; all have full kitchens and private bathrooms. The second-floor Pelican Suite can sleep up to four people. A big upper-floor sun deck overlooking the sea provides the perfect venue from which to watch humpback whales pass by in the winter. A new onsite cafe, **The Little Hut,** is open from noon to 8pm daily, serving light meals, panini, and cappuccinos.

Front St. (P.O. Box 9), Grand Turk, Turks and Caicos, B.W.I. Ⓒ/fax **649/946-2827.** www.grandturkinn.com. 5 units. Winter $300 double; $250 off-season. Rates include continental breakfast. AE, DISC, MC, V. No children 15 or under. **Amenities:** Bikes; Wi-Fi. *In room:* A/C, ceiling fan, TV/DVD, hair dryer, kitchen, Wi-Fi.

Island House On a breezy site overlooking North Creek, this inn was the creation of the late Colin Brooker, a charming English expat, and his Grand Turk–born wife, Lucy. The inn has undergone major renovations since Hurricane Ike. The complex's architectural style evokes the Mediterranean, with rooms opening onto water views. The five one-bedroom suites and three studios are comfortable but nothing fancy; all have kitchens and balconies with sumptuous views overlooking the water and the well-planted gardens. It's not on the beach, but you can easily get there by one of the vehicles provided for guests. The freshwater pool is pillowed in tropical vegetation—an idyllic spot to relax at the end of the day. The hotel staff is happy to arrange any number of outdoor activities, such as diving or snorkeling, kayaking, horseback riding, and fishing.

Lighthouse Rd. (P.O. Box 36), Grand Turk, Turks and Caicos, B.W.I. Ⓒ **649/946-1519.** Fax 649/946-1388. www.islandhouse-tci.com. 8 units. Suites: Winter (2-night package) $240 double nondiver, $315 double diver; off-season (2-night package) $224 double nondiver, $299 double diver. Studios: Winter (2-night package) $208 double nondiver, $283 double diver; off-season $190 double nondiver, $265 double diver. Dive rates include 2 morning boat dives. Children 11 and under stay free in parent's room. Rates include personal use of vehicle and round-trip airport transfers on stays of 4 nights or more. AE, MC, V. **Amenities:** Babysitting; bikes; outdoor freshwater pool; watersports equipment (extensive). *In room:* A/C, ceiling fan, TV, kitchen, hair dryer, Wi-Fi (free).

Manta House You can't ask for a better location than that enjoyed by this fun little pink clapboard B&B, a favorite of divers—only quiet Duke Street, a white picket fence, and a small stretch of sand separate the house from the big blue sea. The entire B&B has been handsomely refurbished, with spiffy new bathrooms and a softer, more

Raking & Making Salt

The large, shallow, stone-bordered ponds in the middle of Grand Turk are not just nesting sites for flamingos and other brilliant birds: They are **salinas,** abandoned artifacts of the salt industry, which ruled the Grand Turk and Salt Cay economies for 300 years. The salt industry began with seasonal salt-rakers coming to the TCI from Bermuda in the late 1600s and lasted until commercial exploitation of the salinas ended in the 1960s. Grand Turk and Salt Cay, the original salt-producing islands, have several natural, shallow, inland depressions (salinas) that filled with salt water directly from the sea or percolated up from underlying rock. Bermudians improved the natural salinas, making them into rock-bordered salt pans or ponds. Salt was made by letting seawater into the salinas through sluice gates located at the beach. Water was concentrated by evaporation in one pond, then concentrated again in a second. The slushy brine was then let into smaller drying pans, where the salt crystallized. The cycle took about 90 days from start to finish, but "crops" for each set of pans were spaced by the individual stages into 20- to 30-day periods. Workers raked the crystallized salt into piles and shoveled it into wheelbarrows. Raking salt under the midday sun was an incredibly labor-intensive business, and many who worked the salt (including a number of slaves) were felled by the brutal conditions.

Who used all this salt? From the time of the first European settlements in North America to the middle of the 1800s, salt was a critical food-preservation item. The United States was dependent upon salt imports to some degree until almost the end of the 19th century. The relative importance of the Turks islands, however, dwindled as the demand for salt expanded. Dwarfed by the demand and other producers and unable to expand pond acreage, mechanize loading, or achieve economies of scale, the salt industry in the Turks islands finally collapsed in the 1960s after 300 years of production.

—*Courtesy of the Turks & Caicos National Museum*

elegant palette. Manta House features three sprawling, self-contained bungalows. The North Bungalow, with two bedrooms and two bathrooms, has a full kitchen and two private patios. The Jungle Bungalow is a one-bedroom, one bathroom suite with its own living room and private patios. The Guesthouse is a 1-, 2-, or 3-bedroom configuration with a full kitchen, a living room, and a private deck.

Duke St. (P.O. Box 222), Grand Turk, Turks and Caicos, B.W.I. ℂ **649/946-1111.** www. grandturk-mantahouse.com. 3–5 units. Winter $1,100–$2,100 per week bungalow, $130–$145 per night double; off-season $995–$1,900 per week bungalow, $110–$125 per night double. Dive packages $75 per person per day. Rates include continental breakfast. MC, V. **Amenities:** Dive packages. *In room:* A/C, TV, kitchen (in North Bungalow and the Guesthouse).

Osprey Beach Hotel ★ Ⓥalue   This landmark hotel was one of the few places on Grand Turk relatively unscathed from Hurricane Ike in late 2008. It has a lovely white-sand-beach setting that offers swimming and snorkeling. Twenty-seven refurbished rooms occupy modern two-story town houses, each with oceanfront verandas; 10 spacious units are located across the street in the Atrium. All of the Queen suites have full kitchens; the rest have kitchenettes or minifridges. Rooms on the upper floors are larger and have higher ceilings, and many have lovely, unobstructed views of the turquoise sea. The lower rooms have easy access to the beach. Lunch and dinner are served poolside (the menu features seafood, steaks, and local favorites like conch chowder); also poolside is the popular **Birdcage Bar.** Newly opened in 2010 is **Joan's Deli and Boutique,** with specialty sandwiches, wraps, salads, and coffees served by the capable Joan from Captain Zheng's (see "Dining," below); it's located in the Atrium. On Sunday and Wednesday nights, the whole of Duke Street and beyond congregates for the **poolside barbecue buffet** ($14–$30) and the toe-tapping ripsaw music of "dive-master troubadour" Mitch Rolling and the High Tide.

Duke St. (P.O. Box 216), Grand Turk, Turks and Caicos, B.W.I. ℂ **649/946-2666.** Fax 649/946-2817. www.ospreybeachhotel.com. 37 units. High season $195–$235 double, $115–$150 courtyard rooms (in Atrium); off-season $165–$190 double, $100–$135 courtyard rooms (in Atrium). Extra person $30 per day. Children 11 and under stay free in parent's room. Dive/hotel packages available. AE, MC, V. **Amenities:** 2 restaurants; bar; outdoor pool; watersports equipment; Wi-Fi (around pool and restaurant; free). *In room:* A/C, ceiling fan, TV, fridge, kitchenette (in some).

The Salt Raker Inn   Once the home of a shipwright who emigrated here from Bermuda, this inn—one of the most historic on the islands—dates from the early 1800s. Today it's been converted into a small inn with a popular local restaurant in the **Secret Garden** (see "Dining," below) and a genial owner. The inn stands right across the street from a good beach of golden sand—which turned out to not be the best location after a major hurricane struck; the inn was still undergoing major renovations (including a new roof) at press time. It should be fully operational by the time this book is published. The Secret Garden is up and running, however, refurbished top to bottom but still set in a garden of tropical foliage (concrete bar this time, not wooden). The Salt Raker has a certain rough-hewn charm—here's hoping the renovations will give the rooms the refreshment they needed even before the hurricane hit. The best rooms are the upstairs suites, which share a breezy balcony with hammocks and sea views.

1 Duke St., Grand Turk, Turks and Caicos, B.W.I. © **649/946-2260.** Fax 649/946-2263. www.hotelsaltraker.com. 12 units. Double $115–$125. MC, V. **Amenities:** Restaurant/bar; babysitting. *In room:* A/C, TV.

DINING

Pirate's Choice Rum Bar & Restaurant, a new restaurant at the White Sands Beach Resort (www.whitesandsbeachresorttci.com), near the cruise terminal, has been stirring up some serious buzz with its fresh mojitos, cracked conch, live music—and a prime location on a scenic Grand Turk beach. Don't miss the **Wednesday-** and **Sunday-night poolside barbecues** at the **Birdcage,** in the Osprey Beach Hotel on Duke Street. The restaurant is also open for dinner (© **649/946-2666**).

You may not want to kill time at the Grand Turk airport—but given certain airlines' island-time mentality, you may be forced to. There's a silver lining, however: the airport restaurant. The **Cockpit Lounge** has surprisingly good island food (it feeds a lot of government officials traveling to and from Cockburn Town), including cracked conch, fish and fries, garlic shrimp, and more (© **649/946-1095;** open Mon–Sat 6am–9pm, Sun 6am–8:30pm; main courses

Dining in Margaritaville

Jimmy Buffett's Margaritaville in the Grand Turk Cruise Center is an impressive sight, as well it should be: It's the largest stand-alone Margaritaville in the entire Caribbean. Its 1486 sq. m (16,000 sq. ft.) can feed up to 500 folks. The colorful, vintage-Bermudian–style restaurant is bordered by a large, lagoon-like pool with a swim-up bar, slide, and infinity edge. It's open only on days when ships come in (4–6 days a week), but that may change. Contact the cruise center at © **649/946-1040** for information about restaurant hours and opening times.

| (Tips) **Shopping for Self-Catering**

Many resorts and rented villas have full kitchens for **self-catering.** You can get all your basic provisions (food, drinks, snacks, toiletries, even fishing gear) at **Cee's Superstore** (Pond Rd.; ☎ **649/946-2995**). **Dot's Food Fair** (Hospital Rd.; ☎ **649/946-2324**), located in the old town center, also offers a grocery/basic provisions store as well as a boutique with toiletries, books, clothes, you name it. Buy **fresh fish** straight off the dock on Front Street when fishermen come in at the end of the day. Liquor, beer, and wine can be bought at any grocery or convenience store (except on Sun) or at **Dot's Liquors** (yes, the very same Dot of Dot's Food Fair), across from the Red Salina on Pond Street.

$10–$20, sandwiches and burgers $4–$9, salads $5–$15. The restaurant also offers Internet access.

Captain Zheng's CHINESE   This hot spot brings 'em in with delicious, freshly made Chinese dishes. You'll dine amid softly draped linens and Oriental lanterns. The menu changes regularly, but among the most popular items are Szechuan chili mountain chicken, garlic shrimp and squid, and Peking duck. As the menu says, no MSG!

At the Salina Houses, Close Haul Rd. (south of Duke St.). ☎ **649/242-2436.** Main courses $11–$23 (Peking duck $30). No credit cards. Tues–Sat 6–10pm.

Jack's Shack Beach Bar & Grill CARIBBEAN   Just north of the cruise port, Jack's is a fun spot to spend a beach day, with lounge chairs, floats, a volleyball net, tantalizing barbecue scents, spine-stiffening rum drinks, and a companionable island vibe. The chef serves up tasty jerk chicken, fish stew, steamed conch, and other local specialties. It's open only those days when cruise ships are in port.

South Base (500m/1640 ft. north of the cruise center). ☎ **649/232-0099.** www.jacksshack.tc. Main courses $5–$12. MC, V. Open only when cruise ships are in (7am–7pm).

The Sandbar CARIBBEAN/WESTERN   This casual, friendly watering hole set above the beach survived Hurricane Ike, and it's back in business as a social hub for locals and visitors and a dog or two lying in the cool sand. It's owned by two vivacious and energetic Canadian sisters, Tonya and Katya, who also run the **Manta House B&B** (☎ **649/946-1111;** www.grandturk-mantahouse.com) across the street. The menu is much more interesting than a beach bar's needs to be, with lobster quesadilla, cracked conch, shrimp and chips, and very respectable burgers.

Duke St. ℂ **649/946-1111.** Main courses $10–$18. MC, V. Sun–Fri noon–late (food served noon–3pm and 6–9pm).

Secret Garden SEAFOOD/CARIBBEAN   Tucked in the covered backyard garden of the Salt Raker Inn (see above), this casual eatery is a local favorite. Flattened by Hurricane Ike, it's been rebuilt (this time with concrete underpinnings), but has retained its dreamy tropical-garden atmosphere and the same reliable kitchen. Lunch specials are tasty and include grouper sandwich, barbecued chicken, and even a hearty spaghetti Bolognese. In the evening you can start with conch bites and settle on an entree of grouper, seafood pasta, garlic shrimp, cracked conch, or curry goat, with a side of peas 'n' rice, of course.

1 Duke St. ℂ **649/946-2260.** Reservations recommended in winter. Lunch specials $9–$18; dinner $12–$21. MC, V. Tues–Sun 7–10am, noon–2:30pm, and 7–9:30pm.

SCUBA DIVING & SNORKELING ★★★

Some of the finest **scuba diving** in the archipelago is around Grand Turk—in fact, a breathtakingly short .8 to 1.6km (½–1 mile) offshore (a 5- to 10-min. boat ride away). The action is at the **"Wall,"** where the western edges of the island (and its necklace of coral reef) plunge dramatically 2,134m (7,000 ft.) into deep water, actually the leeward side of the Turks Island Passage (also known as the Columbus Passage), which lies between the Turks islands and the Caicos islands. Scuba divers flock here to enjoy panoramic wall dives on the vertical sides of the reefs. The diving sites of the Wall have colorful names like Coral Garden, the Aquarium, the Library, and even McDonald's (for its—what else?—coral arch). Near Governor's Beach (and just onshore from the governor's mansion at Waterloo) is a site called Chief Ministers. You'll see all manner of marine life, from giant manta rays and Nassau groupers to big, voluptuous formations of coral and sponges. You'll even see humpback whales as they migrate south through the Turks Island Passage in the winter.

"See" is the operative word in Grand Turk diving: The visibility can exceed 30m (100 ft.). And you don't have to go deep to encounter impressive marine life—active reef zones begin here at depths of just 9m (30 ft.)—meaning you'll enjoy productive dives in better light and using better air production. The proximity of great diving to the docks also means you don't have to spend hours getting to and from your dives—after an afternoon dive you can be back on land in plenty of time for happy hour.

You can also enjoy one of the underwater world's great experiences: **137**
a **night dive** on the Wall, where, due to bioluminescence, the colors
of the day become the phosphorescent illumination of the night.

Snorkeling is good right off many Grand Turk beaches, including
Governor's Beach, White Sands Beach, and **Pillory Beach** (in front
of the Bohio Dive Resort). Many dive operators also offer snorkeling
trips out to the reef, or, when space allows, take snorkelers out on dive
boats, where you will snorkel in water depths of approximately 8m
(25 ft.). The dive shops discussed below all rent snorkel gear.

One extremely popular snorkeling trip is to uninhabited **Gibbs
Cay,** where you can not only snorkel in clear turquoise shallows but
hand-feed and touch docile stingrays.

Dive Operators

The owners and operators of the following dive companies are experienced divers on the island, and they know where to find marine life
in a kaleidoscope of colors. They work with novices—offering good
beginning courses and training—as well as experienced divers of all
skill levels. Rates below are per person.

Blue Water Divers, on Front Street (℅/fax **649/946-1226;** www.
grandturkscuba.com), offers single dives, PADI registration, and dive
packages, and even runs trips to Salt Cay. These people are top-rate
and will tell you many facts and legends about diving in their country
(like the fact that the highest mountain in the Turks and Caicos is
2,400m/7,872 ft. tall, but only the top 42m/138 ft. are above sea
level!). A single-tank dive costs $45, with a two-tank dive going for
$85; a night dive costs $55. Trips to Salt Cay and Gibbs Cay cost $60.
Full PADI certification is $400. (Mitch Rolling, the Blue Water Divers
dive master, is also the guitarist who plays at the Osprey Beach Hotel
on Sun and Wed barbecue nights with the ripsaw band High Tide.)

Cecil Ingham's Sea Eye Diving, on Duke Street (℅ **649/946-
1407;** www.seaeyediving.com), is convenient to most hotels in town.
It offers two-tank morning dives at $75 to $80. An afternoon single-
tank dive costs $45, and a single-tank night dive goes for $55. Rental
equipment is also available. NAUI and PADI courses at all levels are
offered. A full-certification course goes for $400, including training
equipment and boat checkout dives. Dive packages that include
accommodations can be arranged at a hotel of your choice. Snorkeling and cay trips are available for nondivers.

Oasis Divers, on Duke Street (℅ **649/946-1128;** www.oasisdivers.
com), offers complete dive-master services, with dive adventures
along the Wall, night dives, trips to Gibbs Cay, snorkeling trips, trips
to Salt Cay, and dive/accommodations packages. A morning two-tank
dive costs $86; a night dive is $55. An instruction course and dive

from your resort is $110; a trip to Salt Cay is $50 and a trip to Gibbs Cay is $55.

Grand Turk native Smitty Smith is the expert instructor and guide with **Grand Turk Diving** (✆ **649/946-1559;** www.gtdiving.com), which offers dive/lodging packages, a resort course ($150; equipment included), and full scuba certification ($450; equipment included). Two single-tank morning dives cost $75.

EXPLORING THE ISLAND

People mainly travel to Grand Turk to swim, snorkel, dive, and do nothing but soak up the sun. But now that the cruise ships have arrived, local tour operators are offering a mind-numbing assortment of new activities and tours, including horseback-riding trips, jeep safaris, kayaking trips, and dune-buggy tours.

It's a pleasant bike ride to the Northwest Point to see the cast-iron **Grand Turk Lighthouse,** which was brought in pieces from the United Kingdom, where it had been constructed in 1852. Its old lens is on display in the Turks & Caicos National Museum.

Conch World Opened in 2009, this combination theme park, commercial conch farm, and educational complex is located in what was described by one local as a "way-off-the-beaten-path" spot along bumpy dirt roads; the only marking is an arrow pointing the way. Conch World is generally only open when cruise ships are in port. It features a video on the history of the conch in the TCI; some 200 onshore holding tanks containing juvenile conch of different ages; and the full-grown conchs Sally and Jerry, transferred here after a hurricane leveled its sister conch farm in Provo. The complex also includes the Pink Pearl Gift Shop and the Bare Naked Conch Cafe.
South Creek Sound. ✆ **649/946-1228.** Tour $17.

Grand Turk Cruise Center Grand Turk's inaugural season as a Caribbean cruise-ship destination saw some 136 cruise ship calls and 300,000 passengers arrive on the island—and those numbers nearly doubled in 2009. The 5.7-hectare (14-acre) cruise-ship terminal is a fair distance away from the heart of Cockburn Town. The terminal was designed by the folks at Carnival Cruise Lines to resemble a colorful Bermudian-style village out of the early 19th century, much like Cockburn Town might have looked in the early 1800s. The center is planted smack-dab on Governor's Beach, with a 172m-long (565-ft.) main pier; hundreds of deck chairs along the beach; a huge Jimmy Buffet's Margaritaville (with lagoonlike pool and private poolside cabanas); and the Grand Turk FlowRider—a fast-moving artificial-wave pool. The terminal's main building is distinguished by four prominent vintage-style chimneys and shops designed to resemble the quaint wooden salt houses of the salt era—many of which are locally owned and sell island crafts and gifts. It all lies mute and still until the arrival of a 2,000-passenger ship, which shows up on the empty horizon just as the sun comes up—a watery behemoth that gets eye-poppingly bigger as it approaches this tiny island. A miniature train takes arriving cruise passengers to Governor's Beach, or they can choose one of the myriad activities created for them: seeing Cockburn Town by beach buggy, horse-drawn carriage, moped, or shuttle taxi. Or they can participate in one of many shore excursions (scuba diving, snorkeling, horseback riding) available through local tour operators and purchased through the cruise line. Independent-minded travelers who prefer to explore the island on their own can rent a car at the Cruise Center's car-rental office or hire one of the local taxi drivers to give them a tour. *Note:* The cruise center is open only on days when ships come in (now averaging 4–5 days a week).

Waterloo Rd. ✆ **649/946-1040.** www.grandturkcc.com.

Turks & Caicos National Museum ★

This is the country's first (and only) museum. It occupies a 150-year-old residence, Guinep House, originally built by Bermudian wreckers from timbers they salvaged from ships that crashed on nearby reefs. Today about half of its display areas are devoted to the remains of the most complete archaeological excavation ever performed in the West Indies, the wreck of a Spanish caravel (sailing ship) that sank in shallow water sometime before 1513. Used to transport local Lucayans who had been enslaved, the boat was designed solely for exploration purposes and is similar to vessels built in Spain and Portugal during the 1400s.

Treasure hunters found the wreck and announced that it was Columbus's *Pinta* in order to attract financial backers for their salvage—to guarantee a value to the otherwise valueless iron artifacts, in case there proved to be no gold onboard. There is no proof, however, that the *Pinta* ever came back to the New World after returning to Spain from the first voyage. Researchers from the Institute of Nautical Archaeology at Texas A&M University began excavations in 1982, although staff members never assumed that the wreck was the *Pinta*. Today the remains are referred to simply as the Wreck of Molasses Reef.

Although only 2% of the hull now remains intact, the exhibits contain a rich legacy of the everyday (nonbiodegradable) objects used by the crews and officers.

The remainder of the museum is devoted to exhibits about the island's salt industries, its plantation economy, the pre-Columbian inhabitants of the island, and its natural history. The natural-history exhibit features a 2×6m (6½×20-ft.), three-dimensional reproduction of a section of the Grand Turk Wall, the famous vertical reef. You'll

Rippin' Ripsaw

Attend the poolside barbecue at the Osprey Beach Hotel, held every Sunday and Wednesday night, and you'll find yourself enjoying more than the excellent buffet of local dishes. Mitch Rolling and the High Tide play music with a uniquely infectious beat that can't help but get your toes tapping (or even, with the encouragement of a few Turk's Head lagers, get up and dance). That beat comes partly from the goatskin drum and maracas being played alongside the guitar-strumming Mitch (dive master for the Blue Water Divers outfit by day); but the sound that crawls right into your nervous system comes from the guy holding that strange but familiar-looking piece of metal against his thigh and drawing another familiar-looking implement across it. He's playing a handsaw by scraping its teeth vigorously with the shaft of a long-handled screwdriver (the blade of an old knife can also be used). The result is a wonderful, rasping sound that turns any song, from a pop standard to traditional island music, into a rocking, calypso-style dance tune.

Ripsaw music, also known as "rake and scrape," is the national music of Turks and Caicos, and it can be heard across the archipelago. Playing a ripsaw is harder than it looks: Neophytes find their arms and wrists tiring after just a few minutes, but with practice, ripsaw players learn to sustain their art for a full 2- or 3-hour show. The origins of ripsaw are unclear. Some say the art form was brought back to the islands by Belongers who fell in love with a similar style of music played in Haiti and the Dominican Republic and used locally available tools to re-create the rhythms here. Others surmise that the instrumental style was brought here by slaves of Loyalists fleeing the American Revolution. Whatever its roots, it's a style you're sure to fall in love with, too.

also find displays on the geology of the islands and information on the reef and coral growth.

Guinep House, Front St., Cockburn Town, Grand Turk. ✆ **649/946-2160.** www.tc museum.org. Admission $5 nonresidents, free for full-time island residents. Mon–Sat 9am–1pm.

Waterloo Golf Club   Former TCI governor John Kelly loved golf so much he designed and actually helped build this 9-hole course on the grounds of the governor's mansion (Waterloo) and office—it was opened in 1998. Now anyone can play here; call to reserve your tee time. A new clubhouse is in the works.

Waterloo Rd. © **649/946-2308.** Greens fees $25 per day.

GRAND TURK AFTER DARK

At the previously recommended **Osprey Beach Hotel,** on Duke Street (© **649/946-2666**), Wednesday and Sunday barbecues feature music by Mitch Rolling and the High Tide (see below).

2 SALT CAY ★★

When they *really* want to relax, the stressed-out denizens of Grand Turk head to sleepy Salt Cay (pop. 60), for a sundowner, perhaps, at the Coral Reef Bar & Grill, where you might spy a humpback whale from your barstool perch. As one Grand Turker put it: "Salt Cay has two speeds: slow and stop."

Salt Cay's slogan is "The Land that Time Forgot," and if you arrive by air, you'll get the idea. Civilization seems far, far away as you take in the lay of the land on the fly-in: the tiny (2.6 sq. km/1 sq. mile), rural landscape, dotted with abandoned salinas and old windmills, sunbaked remnants of the Bermudian salt-rakers' heyday on the island in the early 19th century, and donkeys and cows ambling down dirt roads. The one-room airport looks like a Wild West storefront, complete with hitching post. It's a wonder you don't head home on the next flight out.

But don't. Give this, the southernmost cay of the Turks islands, a couple of days, at the very least. Grab a snorkel and flippers and dip into the sea right off the beach. Have a lively lunch at Island Thyme Bistro and gaze at the Haitian art papering the walls. Find a message in a bottle lying on the beach. Swim with whales (or stingrays if you prefer). Or just find yourself a hammock or a prime spot on the sugary-sand beach and enjoy one of the most tranquil places you'll ever experience.

ESSENTIALS
VISITOR INFORMATION

Salt Cay has its own very informative website (**www.saltcay.org**), which has a business directory—with listings of accommodations, restaurants, grocery stores, watersports operators, golf-cart rentals, and the like—a map of the island, history, and much more.

Porter Williams's Favorite TCI Experiences

Porter Williams, the owner of Island Thyme Bistro and tireless promoter of all things Salt Cay, first came to the island in the mid-1990s. It was during his first visit to Salt Cay, Porter says, that he became part and parcel of the community. After years of being guests, he and his wife decided that they wanted their children to grow up island-style. They bought a historic structure, and, with the help of local craftsmen, created Island Thyme Bistro. Since then, Porter has danced with Miss Alice at the Senior Citizen's Ball, was Santa at the annual children's Christmas Party, learned to make johnnycakes from Miss Nettie, and dived with manta rays. Here are Porter Williams's favorite TCI experiences:

• Attending glowworm parties.
• Snorkeling for conch and swimming with whales.
• Sampling cracked conch at **Pat's Place** (p. 145).
• Enjoying a margarita at the **Coral Reef Bar & Grill** (Deane's Dock area; ☎ 649/946-6940).
• Walking on a deserted beach.
• Exploring and looking for treasure.
• Visiting with old and new friends.
• Looking at the stars.
• Enjoying the ultimate freedom of living in a place where everyone is accepted and becomes part of the community.

Salt Cay has a handful of grocery/convenience stores, among them **Nettie's Store** and **Pat's Store.** Nettie Talbot, born and bred on Salt Cay, sells fresh-baked bread out of her store.

Getting to Salt Cay

The notoriously tiny airstrip at the Salt Cay airport has been lengthened and resurfaced—but you still need to arrive during daylight hours; the airstrip is not lighted for night. **Air Turks & Caicos** (☎ 649/946-4999 or 649/946-6940 or -6906 on Salt Cay; www.airturksandcaicos.com) and fly to Salt Cay from Providenciales. Or you can charter a flight with **Global Airways** (☎ 649/231-0045; www.globalairways.tc) or **Caicos Express** (☎ 649/244-1407; caicos expressairways@tciway.tc); flights run from $500 to $650 a charter.

ATTRACTIONS ●
White House **4**

ACCOMMODATIONS ■
Charming House Villa **3**
Half Way House **5**
Pirate's Hideaway **1**
Tradewinds Guest Suites **8**
Villas of Salt Cay **6**

DINING ◆
Coral Reef **9**
Pat's Place **2**
Porter's Island Thyme **7**

Air Turks & Caicos offers daily flights between Provo and Salt Cay; the flight takes 30 minutes and costs $160. Contact Global for schedules and fees.

A government-subsidized **ferry** runs between Grand Turk and Salt Cay, weather permitting, every Tuesday, Wednesday, and Friday (leaving from South Dock—the island's *only* dock, by the way). The trip takes an hour and costs $12. You can also hire a **private boat operator** to take you between Salt Cay and Grand Turk (as long as the seas aren't too rough). Contact **Salt Cay Adventure Tours** (© 649/946-6909; www.saltcaytours.com). **Cruise-ship passengers** who arrive in Grand Turk can also contact Salt Cay Adventure Tours to arrange day trips to Salt Cay.

Getting Around Salt Cay

No one needs a car to get around Salt Cay, which has more donkeys than cars; it's the perfect place for getting around on foot, by bike, or by golf cart. Contact **Salt Cay Riders Golf Cart Rentals** (© 649/244-1407; two-seater golf carts $65/day, $350/week; credit cards accepted).

WHERE TO STAY IN SALT CAY

The whimsical and wonderful **Windmills Plantation** did not survive the hurricanes of 2008. The resort had been in operation since 1980, its construction the stuff of a fascinating book, *The Carnival Never Got Started,* by the man who built it, Guy Lovelace. What remains is a 2½-mile span of beachfront along North Beach, one of the best beaches on the island and a top snorkeling spot.

At press time the planned construction of a luxury resort and 18-hole championship golf course was on hold. The locals, who've seen this kind of thing come and go before, are circumspect. As one local put it, "In the Caribbean talk is cheap and construction materials aren't."

Pirate's Hideaway This little guesthouse has two full-service suites and Blackbeard's Quarters, a four-bedroom house that's perfect for families—one bedroom has bunk beds. It has a tropical garden and a freshwater pool. Pirate's Hideaway is a block away from the beach.

Victoria St., Salt Cay, Turks and Caicos, B.W.I. ©/fax **649/946-6909.** www.pirates hideaway.com. 3 units. Suite $200–$225; Blackbeard's Quarters $400. Dive packages available. MC, V. **Amenities:** Freshwater pool. *In room:* A/C, ceiling fan, kitchenette (Blackbeard's Quarters only).

Tradewinds Guest Suites Tradewinds offers five one-bedroom self-catering suites steps away from a lovely beach shaded by casuarina trees. Each suite has a kitchen or kitchenette, bedroom, living room

A Villa Stay in Salt Cay

The island has a number of **villas and cottages** to rent. New to the scene is the waterfront **Villas of Salt Cay** (Historic Victoria St.; ℭ **772/713-9502;** www.villasofsaltcay.com; $300–$475/night high season; $150–$240/night low season). There are three lodging options: the Villa Frangipani, a two-story island home that accommodates six people; the Villa Olivewood, an efficiency apartment that accommodates four; and the Cabanas of the Villas, three connected one-room efficiencies. All three villas are set in a private walled compound ringing a freshwater pool, and all three open onto a deck that overlooks the ocean.

Sink into historic Salt Cay in the handsomely restored and beautifully furnished British-Colonial **Half Way House** (ℭ **561/835-9237;** www.halfwayhousesaltcay.com; $4,800/week high season; $3,900/week low season). It has three bedrooms, two-and-a-half bathrooms, and breathtaking views of the sea.

Watch the whales from your deck at **Charming House Villa** (ℭ **772/713-9502;** www.charminghousevilla.com; $425/night high season; $212–$315/night off-season). This traditional two-story Bermudan Cape was once the home of beloved Salt Cay Belonger Felix Lightbourne. It accommodates six people and has three bedrooms, two bathrooms, and a fully equipped kitchen.

For an updated directory of Salt Cay villas, go to **www.saltcay.org**.

with a sofa bed, private bathroom, and a screened porch. You can ask the staff to stock food for your arrival, or choose an all-inclusive meal and dive package.

Victoria St., Salt Cay, Turks and Caicos, B.W.I. ℭ **649/946-6906.** Fax 649/946-6940. www.tradewinds.tc. 5 units. Winter $161–$190 single or double; off-season $133–$161 single or double. Each additional person up to 4 people $20 per night. Children 11 and under free. Weekly rates available. Ask about meal and dive packages. MC, V. **Amenities:** Bikes; barbecue grills; hammocks. *In room:* A/C on request, ceiling fan, kitchen/kitchenette.

WHERE TO DINE IN SALT CAY

Pat's Place ★ ISLAND Pat Simmons is a retired schoolteacher (she taught for 28 years in the Salt Cay school system) who now runs this modest eatery out of her home, on a latticed screened-in patio with yellow walls, green trim, and bright-colored tablecloths. Call ahead to say you're coming, give Pat your order, and when you arrive, you'll be treated to delicious island food served family-style. Choose from steamed or fried fish, curry conch, barbecued chicken, peas 'n' rice, greens, and more. Beer and wine are available.

Historic South District. ℂ **649/946-6919.** Reservations required for all meals. $15 per person dinner without beer or wine. No credit cards. Daily 7:30am–9:30pm.

Porter's Island Thyme ★ CARIBBEAN/INTERNATIONAL   If this is the nerve center of Salt Cay, then its ebullient owner, Porter Williams, is its commander. The Island Thyme is more than just a good place to eat—it's the local bank, the Wi-Fi center, and party central. Where else can you sip a cool Cuba Libre while cheering on a hermit crab race? Where else can you dine out on filet mignon and shrimp scampi, smoke a fine Cuban cigar, and then walk home under a canopy of stars in your bare feet? Porter Williams brings together the widely disparate passions of his life in this delightful restaurant, and visitors are the better for it. Island Thyme is open for breakfast, lunch, and dinner and has a lively bar scene—ask about the Wolf shooter, but sign over everything you own to a trusted family member before imbibing. At night, sample such delicacies as coconut shrimp, almond-crusted snapper, duck breast au Grand Marnier, and seafood paella. See you at Friday Pizza Night!

Salt Cay. ℂ **649/242-0325** or 649/343-2155. www.islandthyme.tc. Main courses $18–$35 (seafood paella for two or three: $51). MC, V. Daily 7–9am, noon–2pm, and 6:30–9pm. Closed 1 day a week in the off-season and 2 months a year (generally May and mid-Oct through mid-Nov).

EXPLORING SALT CAY

Aside from the salinas, some interesting architecture remains from the salt-raking days of the early 19th century. The 1834 stone-and-stucco **White House** was the home of a Bermudian salt-raker; the downstairs is a salt warehouse (tour by appointment only).

The 200-year-old **Government House** has been acquired by the Turks & Caicos National Trust, which plans to restore this historic property, once the seat of government for the island. For more information, go to **http://saltcaypreservation.org**.

Salt Cay Adventure Tours (ℂ **649/946-6909;** www.saltcaytours. com) is an all-purpose watersports activities operator. They can arrange scuba-diving trips (for a fully equipped PADI dive shop, see **Salt Cay Divers,** below), guide you on snorkeling, whale-watching, or snorkeling adventures, rent out bikes and kayaks, and will do island-history and art tours. **Cruise-ship passengers** who arrive in Grand Turk can also contact Salt Cay Adventures to arrange day trips to Salt Cay.

Diving Salt Cay's Walls

The Northwest Wall, Kelly's Folly, and Turtle Garden offer wall diving at its finest—and each of these dive sites is just 5 to 10 minutes from the Salt Cay dock. Huge gorgonians, soft coral, and sponges form a backdrop for a family of spotted eagle rays, turtles, pelagics, and dolphins. A green moray eel whose head is at least .3m (1 ft.) high, his huge body and tail wrapped in and out of a rock formation, can often be seen at Northwest Wall and Rockery. Divers can observe conch working their way up a timeworn trail on the wall. Night-dive with fluorescent strings of pearls threading their way through the water, sleeping turtles, slipper lobsters, huge crabs, nurse sharks, and a seasonal array of other night critters.

—*Michele Belanger-McNair and Debbie Been, Salt Cay Divers*

Scuba Diving ★★

Divers can explore the wreck of the **HMS *Endymion*** ★ off Salt Cay, which went down in a storm in 1790. Two centuries later, Brian Sheedy, a local diver and inn operator, discovered the wreck. Today, while the reef has reclaimed the hull and all else that was biodegradable, divers can still get a close-up look at its 18 coral- and sponge-encrusted cannons and nine huge anchors lying about. Resting in just 12m (40 ft.) of water, it's one of the region's most popular snorkel and dive sites.

A fully equipped PADI dive shop with instruction at every level, **Salt Cay Divers** (© **649/946-6906;** www.saltcaydivers.tc) offers scuba divers small groups and personalized service. Children can learn to dive in the Bubble Maker program while Mom and Dad get their certification or advanced rating. Carolina skiffs are able to get up close to prime reefs and dive sites, and a 9.8m (32-ft.) V-hull is used for longer, smoother rides to other islands and cays. Salt Cay Divers regularly dives South Caicos's reefs as well as Grand Turk's dive sites. Ask about hotel/dive packages. Salt Cay Divers also offers snorkeling and whale-watching trips.

Snorkeling ★★

As good as the diving is on Salt Cay, it may be an even better snorkeling destination; the island, in fact, has some of the best snorkeling in the TCI, and you can do most of it right off the beaches. The **Bluff,**

Point Pleasant, and **Aquarium** sites offer opportunities to watch squid, tarpon, barracuda, and colorful coral heads and fans. **Queen's Beach,** on the north shore, is another great spot to see lots of brilliantly hued fish.

Day trips to **Great Sand Cay,** an uninhabited national park, allow picnickers to snorkel, swim, view iguanas and tide pools, and bird-watch. Other uninhabited islands can be visited, such as **Gibbs Cay,** where you can snorkel with stingrays. At **Whale Island** you can walk off the beach with snorkel and mask to see parrotfish and stingrays. Day trips to these cays (as well as overnight trips to Great Sand Cay) can be arranged through Salt Cay Divers (see above).

Whale-Watching ★★★

Between January and April, **humpback whales** come here to play as they travel the 2,134m (7,000-ft.) trench of the Columbus Passage to the Silver Banks to mate and calf. Visitors can watch their antics from shore, boat out among them, or strap on dive or snorkeling equipment and go below. Salt Cay is one of the last places in the world you can actually get in the water and swim with these impressive creatures. Salt Cay Divers (see above) does what is called "soft water encounters." As Debbie Been of Salt Cay Divers explains it: "We gently slide into the water after ensuring that the whales are not frightened by our presence. Then the whales actually swim toward you. We ask that you not get too close, but believe me, those whales know exactly where you are—and if they wanted to hurt you, they would, but they are truly gentle creatures. We snorkel for a few minutes and watch their graceful bodies underwater. The usual encounter only lasts a few minutes, but it's the thrill of a lifetime."

7

Fast Facts

1 FAST FACTS: TURKS & CAICOS

AREA CODE   The area/country code for the TCI is **649.**

ATMS & ABMS   **FirstCaribbean** has 24-hour ABM service at the main branches of its bank on Provo, Grand Turk, and South Caicos and a branch in the Saltmills shopping complex on Provo's Grace Bay Road. **Scotiabank** has 24-hour ATMs at Waterloo Plaza on Grand Turk and at four locations on Provo: at the Provo airport check-in hall; at the new Graceway Gourmet on Grace Bay Road; next to the Graceway IGA on Leeward Highway; and at Petro Plus on Millennium Highway. **TCI Bank Limited (TCIB)** has ATMs at its locations in Provo, Grand Turk, and North Caicos. The country's only drive-through ATM is located in Provo's Graceway Plaza in a branch of the **International Banking Group (IBG)** (© **649/941-4424;** www. ibgtci.com).

BANKS   Branches and ATMs of **FirstCaribbean International Bank** (© **649/946-4245;** www.firstcaribbeanbank.com) and **Scotiabank** (© **649/946-4750;** www.scotiabank.com) are at convenient and central locations on both Provo and Grand Turk. The country's first indigenous bank, **TCI Bank Limited (TCIB),** has opened branches on Grand Turk, North Caicos, South Caicos, and Provo's Grace Bay (Regent Village; © **649/941-7500;** www.tcibankltd.com). The islands' newest retail and commercial bank, the **International Banking Group (IBG)** (© **649/941-4424;** www.ibgtci.com), has opened a branch in Provo's Graceway Plaza with the country's only drive-through ATM.

BUSINESS HOURS   Most shops are open Monday to Saturday from 10am to 6pm, but hours vary. Banks are generally open Monday to Thursday from 8:30am to 3pm and Friday from 8:30am to 5pm—although TCI Bank is also open Saturday morning. Most grocery stores are open 7 days a week but do not sell liquor, beer, or wine on Sunday.

CURRENCY   The **U.S. dollar** is the official currency.

DENTISTS **Dental Services Limited** is located in the Medical Building on Leeward Highway in Providenciales (☎ 649/946-4321; www.dentist.tc).

DOCTORS **Dr. Sam Slattery** sees patients at the **Grace Bay Medical Centre** (Neptune Plaza, Allegro Rd., Providenciales; ☎ 649/941-5252; emergencies: 649/231-0525). **Associated Medical Practices** is located in the Medical Building on Leeward Highway in Providenciales (☎ 649/946-4242; emergencies: 649/331-4357; www.doctor.tc). Associated also has a dive recompression chamber.

DRUGSTORES There are two full-service pharmacies: **Grace Bay Pharmacy,** located in Neptune Plaza on Dolphin Drive between Grace Bay Road and the Leeward Highway (☎ 649/946-8242), and **Island Pharmacy,** in the Associated Medical Building on Leeward Highway in Providenciales (☎ 649/946-4150).

ELECTRICITY The electric current on the islands is 120 volts, 60 cycles, AC. European appliances will need adapters.

EMERGENCIES Call ☎ **911** or **999** for an **ambulance,** to report a **fire,** or to contact the **police.**

HOSPITALS & MEDICAL FACILITIES In April 2010, **Turks & Caicos Island Hospital,** the nation's first modern hospital, opened its two centers: the **Cheshire Hall Medical Centre** (on Providenciales) and the **Cockburn Town Medical Center** (on Grand Turk). **Grace Bay Medical Centre** is an urgent-care medical facility in Providenciales (Neptune Plaza, Allegro Rd., Providenciales; ☎ 649/941-5252; for emergencies call ☎ 649/231-0525). **Grand Turk Hospital** is on Hospital Road in Grand Turk (☎ 649/946-2040). The other islands have community clinics.

INTERNET ACCESS Most resorts and hotels have some sort of Internet access. You can also access the Internet at **CompTCI** (Suzy Turn Plaza, Provo; ☎ 649/941-4266; www.comptci.com). Prices are around $10 an hour.

LANGUAGE The official language is English.

PETS All you need to bring a pet onto the islands is a signed veterinary certificate (dated within 1 month of travel) stating that the animal is free of contagious or infectious disease and up-to-date on his or her rabies and distemper vaccinations. There is no quarantine period for incoming pets.

POST OFFICE The Provo Post Office and Philatelic Bureau is located downtown at the corner of Airport Road. It's open Monday to Thursday from 8am to 4pm and Friday from 8am to 3:30pm. The

It's open Monday to Friday from 8am to 4pm.

TAXES   There is a departure tax of $35, payable when you leave the islands (it's often included in the cost of your airfare). The government collects an 11% occupancy tax, applicable to all hotels, guesthouses, and restaurants in the 40-island chain. Resorts generally add a 10% to 15% service charge on top of the government tax.

TELEPHONE   To call Turks and Caicos, dial **1** and then the number. The country code for the TCI is **649.** The international-operator telephone service is ☎ **115.** Local directory assistance is ☎ **118.**

To call a phone carrier in the U.S., dial **0,** then **1,** and then the number. You can make domestic and international calls using your credit card or prepaid phone cards, available in $5, $10, and $15 denominations—although rates for either are often as exorbitant as calling direct from your hotel room (you'll be charged more than $2 a minute, depending on the time of day—and many hotels even charge $1 and up for local calls). Public pay phones accept prepaid phone cards only. You can buy these prepaid phone cards at a number of retail outlets and hotels, including Avis, and Club Med (Provo); Parrot Cay (Caicos Cays); the Middle Caicos Co-op; and the Poop Deck (Grand Turk). If you have a GSM cellphone with international roaming capacity, you can use that on the islands; a money-saving option is to buy or rent a cellphone in the TCI (see the "Calling Home" box in chapter 2).

TIME   The islands are in the Eastern Standard Time zone, and daylight saving time is observed.

TIPPING   Hotels often add 10% to 15% to your bill automatically, to cover service. If individual staff members perform various services for you, it is customary to tip them something extra. If you go on an island tour, watersports charter, or beach excursion, it's always a good idea to tip your guide 10% to 20%, depending on the level of service you receive. In restaurants 15% is appropriate unless a service charge has already been added; if in doubt, ask. Tip taxi drivers 10% to 15%.

WATER   Government officials insist that the water in Turks and Caicos is safe to drink. Nonetheless, stick to bottled water, especially if you have a delicate stomach.

INDEX

See also Accommodations and Restaurant indexes, below.